CHILDREN IN EXILE

CHILDREN IN EXILE

Thekla Clark

Chatto & Windus
LONDON

Published by Chatto & Windus 1998

2 4 6 8 10 9 7 5 3 1

First published in Great Britain in 1998 by
Chatto & Windus
Random House, 20 Vauxhall Bridge Road,
London SW1V 2SA

Random House Australia (Pty) Limited
20 Alfred Street, Milsons Point, Sydney,
New South Wales 2061, Australia

Random House New Zealand Limited
18 Poland Road, Glenfield,
Auckland 10, New Zealand

Random House South Africa (Pty) Limited
Endulini, 5A Jubilee Road, Parktown 2193, South Africa
Random House UK Limited Reg. No.954009

A CIP catalogue record for this book is available from the British Library

ISBN 0 7011 6590 1

Papers used by Random House UK Limited are natural,
recyclable products made from wood grown in sustainable forests.
The manufacturing processes conform to the environmental
regulations of the country of origin.

Typeset by SX Composing DTP, Rayleigh, Essex
Printed and bound in Great Britain by Mackays of Chatham PLC

Dedicated to Sarin Khul
and all the other victims of the Khmer Rouge madness

Grateful thanks to
James Fenton, Darryl Pinckney and Lorna Sage (yet again) for
everything, Lisa Darnell for invaluable suggestions, corrections
and assistance, J.B. the brightest, boldest, most beautiful of
publishers, for taking a chance.

Grateful acknowledgements are made by the publisher and the
author to James Fenton and Penguin Books Ltd for the use of
quotations from his poem 'Children in Exile'.

CONTENTS

PREFACE

My husband John and I are Americans who have lived in Italy for most of our lives. We met in Florence where we had both come to live, he from Georgia, I from Oklahoma. John arrived in 1949 to study Renaissance Philosophy and Art History at the University. He had previously attended an American College whose curriculum consisted of reading 'The Hundred Great Books'. All studies were from original sources, history directly from Herodotus, geometry from Euclid, philosophy from Socrates. When studies leapt from Dante to Machiavelli in one fell swoop John felt he had missed something. He determined to seek out that missing two hundred year gap in Italy.

During our adolescence, war-torn Europe was terra incognita, forbidden, isolated. The opening up of Europe after 1945 was a moment of great exhilaration for all of our generation. Armed with what he called 'The Family Fulbright' of one hundred dollars a month John set out for Florence. With this money he rented a decent flat, ate well in carefully chosen trattorias and was even able to buy books. Most of his fellow students lived on less. The arrangement was clearly temporary and John, never short on ideas, cast about for a more permanent solution to ensure his stay in Italy. His Art History professor (the brilliant and eccentric Roberto Longhi) was enthusiastic about John's plan to create a photographic colour archive of works of art: so enthusiastic he financed the project. This grew into the *Società Scala* and an extensive archive of European works of art. John retired in 1989 because of ill health but *Scala* still flourishes.

I came to Florence in 1953 as a tourist, lost my head over the place, and in 1954 moved here with my daughter Lisa for what was to be a three month visit. I stayed and stayed and stayed. John and I married here in 1961 and our son Simon was born here in 1965. Our work is here, our home is here. We are, however, still bound to America by citizenship, blood ties, tradition and a strong love.

Throughout the sixties we watched with mounting concern as American involvement in Southeast Asia increased. We longed to do something, we didn't know exactly what. We had signed countless petitions, we'd written to a congressman. We'd felt outraged and diminished by American foreign policy. We'd also felt helpless and eventually cobbled together a sort of policy of our own.

We had already tried to make a home for a refugee. Our close friend – a friend so close he is family – the poet James Fenton, was at one time a correspondent in Southeast Asia. In 1973 I asked his help in finding a Vietnamese child we might bring to the West to live with us. He suggested a teenage boy who had acted as an ad hoc interpreter for him. The boy, who was fifteen at the time, was named Lam Xuan Binh. We began to correspond with Binh and even exchanged photographs. However, getting him out of South Vietnam at the time presented a problem. He was almost old enough for military service and the government was desperate for soldiers. The American Consul in Florence did his best and Italian immigration papers were not difficult but the South Vietnamese refused to let him go. His letters were charming and in his photograph he is leaning on a hideous, modern statue of the Virgin Mary in front of the convent where he had gone to school and learned his English. He was a lean, smiling youth carefully dressed in jeans purchased, he wrote us, with one of the cheques we sent him. He also used some of the money to buy English books and wrote, 'I am still your rich boy'. Our correspondence continued for over a year but as he reached his sixteenth birthday our hopes for getting him out diminished. Then the letters stopped and the last cheque was never cashed. James learned later that he had joined the Viet Cong. Still later we heard from Binh's sister that 'our rich boy' had been killed. I cursed the bureaucrats who had kept him back.

In 1975 Saigon fell. We saw photographs of Vietnamese clinging to the helicopters taking Americans to safety and we realized we had lost more than a war. When the opportunity came through the Italian charity *Caritas* to help Vietnamese 'boat people', we felt there was finally something we could do. In 1979 we offered a home to a Vietnamese family and a little over a year later, to the remains of a Cambodian one. We live in a rambling, battered house in the Tuscan countryside. My daughter Lisa was then grown up and Simon was in school in London, so space was no problem. Or perhaps empty space *was* a problem. We'd always had a house full; full of children, full of our friends, Lisa's friends, Simon's friends. We acted on impulse, impulse born of the chagrin we felt at American policies coupled with the human impulse of wanting to help the helpless. In any case the whole thing crept up on us bit by bit. The moment was right, the action now seems inevitable. What it seemed at the time, I, honestly, no longer remember. I suppose we wanted to be good.

We were concerned about what we were taking on, but not really worried. After all we had adapted, painlessly, to another culture. (Florence is quite a distance from Albany, Georgia or Oklahoma City.) But our moves had been simple, from one Indo-European language to another; one form of Christianity to another; a similar climate; a landscape and an architecture we were familiar with from books. And above all there were no closed frontiers, no barbed-wire, no blockades: if we ever wished for another change all we had to do was pack our bags. How could our experience possibly be of use to these people whose main concern was to remain alive, whose knowledge of another world, another culture, another language was almost nil?

There was a great deal we didn't know. We didn't know that hills are frightening, we didn't know that Vietnamese and Cambodians are historic enemies, that most Orientals find milk products nauseating. We had to learn how to provide the right kind of home, a place they could grow into easily and, just as easily, out of. We had to show them that moving held no further terrors and that they were safe at last. We had to learn that our curiosity and their memories weren't always compatible. That it helped to talk but that talk and memory must come when and how it suited them. John and I realized we would have to learn to understand customs, traditions and lives completely different from our own. Even if we were able to take all this in, could we, without personal and emotional knowledge, make use of what we were learning? If we couldn't, how could we possibly be of any real help in the fiendishly difficult business of their adjustment?

This story deals with our education as well as theirs. Similarities in ideas and morality helped us understand each other. Differences, from taste to manners, helped us define each other. For the most part it was good will, on both sides, and what grew into an affection so strong I do not hesitate to call it love. Our horizons and our hearts were enlarged.

PART I

In dangerous camps between facing armies,
  The prey of pirates, raped, plundered or drowned,
In treacherous waters, in single file through the minefields,
  Praying to stave off death till they are found,

Begging for sponsors, begging for a Third Country,
  Begging America to take them in –
It is they, it is they who put everything in hazard.
  What we do decides whether they sink or swim.

IT BEGAN IN 1975 after the fall of Saigon and the end of a war we had opposed from the beginning. The well-publicized plight of the 'boat people' was a further link in a chain of shame and helplessness. My husband, John, and I talked and talked about it, we moaned and commiserated with like-minded friends but we did nothing.

One day John saw a notice in our local Florentine newspaper that the Italian charity *Caritas* was to hold a public meeting to explain what could be done to help the 'boat people'. John went alone to the meeting because we had quarreled, violently, about something that must have seemed important at the time. After the last word is screeched and the final door is slammed, I usually go to bed with a novel. John 'does' something. This time he did indeed do something. The meeting was an avalanche of rhetoric, accusations, counter-claims and *aria fritta* (fried air) from citizens seeking a public forum. Finally John stood up and said that all this talk of political and social position was simply fascinating but what could he personally do to help. The question was asked in all sincerity and it was answered in all practicality. A well-fed, balding priest sitting on the platform said 'See me on your way out'. As he was leaving, John felt a firm hand on his shoulder. It was the chubby determined priest who shoved a piece of paper at him and said 'Just sign here. How many do you want?' Startled, but pleased by something concrete at last, John signed up to offer housing, sustenance and employment to a family of not more than four.

We began to look forward eagerly to the arrival of the refugees. We even practiced – I would be the Vietnamese and John would, by gesture and simple speech make me feel at home. Then we would reverse the roles. We waited and waited but there was only silence. We tried to trace Don Fabrizio (the chubby priest) of *Caritas*, the only name we had, but failed. We waited and in time almost forgot. Months later – John says it was three but I remember it being even longer – we got a card in the mail. It was a printed form that I thought was someone's dental appointment until I noticed that John Clark had been assigned blank blank blank which consisted of blank blank. The spaces had been filled in by hand to tell us that the 'Du Cau family' of 'three units' was now ours. There was no more information.

Again we rang *Caritas*, and this time we were put through to Don Luigi Bartoletti. Don Luigi had become the 'responsabile' (man in charge) of all the Asian refugees in Tuscany. 'Our' family, he told us, was being brought, with a group of other refugees, to a monastery quite near our house and we could go to meet them the day after tomorrow. What, we wondered, did these units consist of – two grandparents and a maiden aunt? Don Luigi assured us that we would be pleased and kept what information he had to himself. A Florentine with a pronounced local accent, Don Luigi had a 'no nonsense' approach that coupled with a salty Tuscan humour left him marginally short of rudeness. It was, we learned, his answer to the chronic disorganization of the volunteers, the charity and Italians in general. It was his method of controlling the love of rhetoric and the unbridled individualism, bordering on anarchy, that surrounded him. Italian benevolence, operatic style and natural wit limit frustration when things don't get done, or at least make the messes more attractive.

It was the middle of a stormy November in 1979 when we

drove the few miles from our house along the deserted, twisting road to *L'Incontro* – a sixteenth-century monastery whose name means 'The Meeting'. Legend has it that Saint Domenic met and lovingly embraced Saint Francis here, a popular subject for Renaissance painters. On a clear day there is a splendid view of the valley of the Arno with the city like a Renaissance painting in the background. A row of cypresses, black against a tempestuous sky, marked the beginning of the monastery. We parked the car and walked towards the only light in view which came from a square, newish building attached to the renovated church. There was no answer to our knock but the door was unlocked so we stepped into an icy corridor, dimly lit but freshly painted. As we walked along we heard noises, noises like spring rain that grew louder, but never loud. Following our ears we came to a large dining room and identified the sound. It was the sound of Asian laughter, which I would come to recognize as a leaven to almost any conversation: embarrassment, doubt, complication, difficulty, bewilderment, mortification and of course, joy were all expressed in that gentle laughter. There were, I learned through the Orientals, moments in which laughter is less callous or heartless than tears.

In the refectory were about twenty Vietnamese of all ages in the middle of an Italian lesson. The teacher, a pretty girl in blue jeans, was as amused and delighted as her pupils. A substantial man who looked, except for his soutane, like my local butcher came over to us. It was Don Luigi. After the ritual exchange of compliments (considerably briefer than usual) he introduced us to 'our family'. Tuyen, the father, was fairly tall, incredibly thin with lank pitch-black hair and the dirty-beige pallor that comes from lack of food. His wife, Trinh, who seemed little more than a child, looked even thinner and her delicate face was tense and strained. Tuyen threw his arms around John in an awkward but deeply moving gesture and buried his head on John's shoulder. We were all surprised, including Tuyen himself. All except Don Luigi who had, he rather condescendingly told us later, the 'advantage of The Faith.' Everyone in the room joined with the general delight and the room itself seemed to rock with Asian laughter. I had felt like a spectator looking through the keyhole but suddenly the doors were flung wide open and Trinh and I kissed unselfconsciously. Trinh knew a few words of English, enough to say 'Thank you for life'. What one answers to that I still don't know. Their smiles and laughter made an answer unnecessary.

We went upstairs to a tiny cell-like room where our third unit, a baby as pale and fragile as a piece of old porcelain, slept with his hands above his head in what I knew from my own children to be the ideal position for tranquil rest. A born baby-snatcher, I left the room with a reluctance that Trinh understood immediately. Our expressions of genuine delight were cut short by Don Luigi who took John aside and said, 'Now what about this job?' I began to feel as though we were trying to join an exclusive club whose membership was already oversubscribed. I found myself apologizing for our simple arrangements but was interrupted by John who is not an easy man to rattle. In his flawless Italian, he convinced Don Luigi of our good intentions. Don Luigi was too much of a Tuscan to express approval and certainly not optimism – a proper Tuscan when asked 'How are you' answers 'Non c'e male' (not too bad) or if he is feeling exceptionally well, 'Bene per ora' meaning alright for now. Whether it was the general atmosphere or John's impeccable accent, I don't know but Don Luigi seemed satisfied enough. After expressions of affection all round and one more look at the baby we left, promising to return in a week (health controls were necessary) to collect 'our' new family and take them home. On the way back John and I kept laughing and congratulating each other, passing our euphoria back and forth as though it were some delectable dish or precious wine. When we got home we each took a stiff drink to sober up.

The move itself was simple as their possessions were few. *Caritas* had explained to us that their eleven-month stay on the infamous Malaysian island of Pulan Bidong had meant that what few valuables they brought with them had disappeared. Ostensibly a haven for refugees, by all accounts Pulan Bidong was more like a concentration camp: the refugees were confined, half-starved and brutalized by Malaysian guards. Tuyen's watch and Trinh's wedding ring had been traded for food and enough plastic to cover the shelter Tuyen had built out of driftwood. Fortunately Trinh had been able to nurse the baby who was only four months old when they left Vietnam. The baby's two cousins who were older (two and four) lost all their teeth and quite a bit of hair from malnutrition.

There are those who believe – like my mother – that sleep is the great healer; I hold with those who favour proper food. We were able to provide both. Recovery came remarkably quickly, and as they began to relax and gain weight it became clear how pretty Trinh was and how attractive Tuyen. The baby was enchanting. When he first came to us he was fifteen months old and not only could he not walk he didn't even have strength enough to sit up. His fontanelle was not closed, and he had no muscular control over his eyes. This was due to malnutrition. A friend who is a doctor later told me that had the baby remained on the island in those conditions that within another three or four months he could have been permanently brain damaged. Instead, within three months he was everywhere, a golden, dimpled delight with even one eye straightened out.

We had, in those days, an Italian couple, Bruno and

Bruna, working for us and living in the house. Their peasant sense of practicality was jolted by our decision to take in the Du Caus but there were never any signs of resentment or jealousy on either part. While continuing to think us quite mad they learned to love the Vietnamese. There were clashes of culture. Both Bruno and Bruna were scandalized by the Oriental method of toilet training. Bo (whose name means precious) ran about with holes in his clothes at the appropriate places, followed closely by his mother with a damp cloth. When Bo caught a cold John and I were amazed to see Trinh scraping an object that looked menacingly like a dragon's tooth. After she had shaved off a number of grains she put them in a brew and fed this to the baby. I do not recommend either practice but must admit that Bo's cold cleared up and that he was toilet trained in record time.

The first winter was harsh and they all suffered. Shots against whooping cough came too late and all three caught it. Trinh had chilblains and Bo had two permanent red circles on his cheeks, like those painted Russian dolls. I realized for the first time just how levelling winter is – how unreliable the sun, how unpredictable the winds, how upsetting the early darkness – especially so for anyone born into a tropical climate. The bareness, the stripping down of colour, the cruel wind, the bitter, bitter cold, surprised and frightened Trinh. 'Will it ever end?' she asked. Then, almost suddenly, the cold ceased, the wind became a breeze, the sun shone through a rip in the sky that widened until it became a dazzling blue with soft white clouds designed to hold the wind in place. I couldn't help feeling that it was our reward. The Vietnamese seemed to draw a deep, inaudible sigh of relief, as though they were finally safe.

Tuyen started work in the laboratory at *Scala* a few weeks after his arrival. At first I drove him to work but at Christmas we gave him a motorbike so that he could feel more independent. I learned later that in those first months his hands were always icy, almost frozen. He knew nothing about gloves; in South Vietnam even coats were a status symbol and not a necessity.

A new language is difficult for almost anyone, for Tuyen it was traumatic. Even after all these years his spoken Italian is atrocious and although he knows and understands the language well he is not easily understood. He had a terrible time that first year. Tuscan humour was a mystery to him, a troublesome one. What was in reality normal banter, heavy-handed but not ill-intentioned, offended his Oriental male pride and he tried to strike back with his limited understanding and even more limited Italian. I was called in to *Scala* to arbitrate. When he tried to plead his own case to me, words failed him and he laid his head down on the table and cried, oh, how he cried! He wept with the abandonment of a child, with a sorrow born of ignorance and loneliness. It was harrowing for us both. Through Don Luigi we found a priest a few hours' drive away who had lived in China and Vietnam and spoke both languages. We took Tuyen to see him in his remote and beautiful country parish. With him was a Chinese nun, elderly and battle scarred. My heart sank as she greeted Tuyen with a barrage of sounds, aggressive even to my unknowing ears. The priest, an elderly, white-haired, soft spoken man in carpet slippers and a shawl around his shoulders, raised a delicate, blue-veined hand and turned her off like a tap. He then talked to Tuyen, softly and soberly. Soberly, until he brought out a bottle of fiery liquor that he had distilled himself, an Italian adaptation of the Chinese Mai Tai. I forced down a small part of my glass. Tuyen and the priest each had two and we left after almost an hour, reeling and smiling. Whether it was the priest's encouragement, time and knowledge or basic Italian humanity I don't know, but within a few months it all straightened

9

out. Even today Tuyen is still friends with some of his ex-colleagues, all differences long forgotten.

It was easier for Trinh who spoke a few words of English and did well in her Italian lessons. She and I would meet everyday for an hour's talk and language practice and within a short time we were able to have a proper conversation. It was in this way that Trinh was able to tell me the story of her family.

Trinh's family name was Van: her father, Xiem Thang Van had fled to Vietnam in the face of the Japanese invasion of China in the thirties, the first in a long line of family refugees. He lived through the Japanese conquest of Indochina and the French occupation that followed. The French rulers created the State of Vietnam with the former Emperor Bao Dai as head of state. The defeat of the French by Vietnamese forces at the battle of Dien Bien Phu on May 7, 1954, ended French domination. An international peace conference was immediately called in Geneva. The treaty signed there called for temporary partition of the country, to be followed by elections in 1956, when the Vietnamese would decide their own government.

The 1954 Geneva Peace Accord seemed to presage a better future for the country, and for Xiem as well, who was working as a baker in the southern town of Chau-Doc, almost at the Cambodian border. In 1955 he met his future wife and his fortunes changed definitively. Because he had been born in China he was accepted as a son-in-law by a rich Chinese/Vietnamese family. (Those Chinese coming directly from the Middle Kingdom were considered superior to those born locally.) Xiem's father-in-law controlled a large portion of river traffic and owned a fleet of small boats. The young family (Trinh as the eldest was born in Chau-Doc in 1956) moved to a village on the Xa No River, a tributary of the Mekong, shortly after the birth of the second child in 1957.

Meanwhile in Saigon, Ngo Dinh Diem, the Prime Minister under the sybaritic Bao Dai, was busy consolidating his personal power and doing his best to thwart the Geneva Peace Accord. The United States supported Diem in blocking the implementation of the elections – elections that seemed certain to be won by the Communists. An experienced anti-French and anti-Communist politician, Diem seemed to be the man who could best advance America's interests in the region. The magnitude of Washington's mistaken judgment is now easily apparent. That the direction of an important phase in American History could be shaped by the strength and weakness of this one man seemed impossible but as American involvement in Vietnam increased this became more and more evident.

The father-in-law had left the river traffic in Xiem's hands and moved to Saigon as an adviser to the last of the Nguyen rulers, Bao Dai. He had long been an important member of the Hoa Hao sect. Ostensibly a religious offshoot of Buddhism, the sect, like the larger Cao Dai Catholic movement, became in effect a private army at the service of the highest bidder. The sect had collaborated with the Japanese and received French funding and support. The founder of the Hoa Hao, a faith-healer named Huynh Phu So, was murdered by the Communists in 1947. From then on the Hoa Hao army of an estimated 15,000 men retaliated by killing Communists in the western Mekong Delta. Instead of forging an alliance, Diem set out to destroy them, convinced that, at the time, pro-French forces were more of a menace to his power than the Communists. Sustained by American military and economic aid he reigned in the Cao Dai, the Binh Xuyen (an organized criminal society) and Hoa Hao armies. One of the Hoa Hao leaders was caught and guillotined publicly in Can Tho. Diem then dethroned Bao Dai. Now firmly in power Diem proclaimed the Republic of Vietnam (RVN) at the end of 1955. In the name of the Republic he passed laws ordering arrest and detention of any person he deemed a menace to security. Later the laws were enlarged to permit execution as well, even on suspicion. Diem had devised an exotic philosophy of his own: a mixture of Catholic, Confucian and Indian concepts cemented by his admiration of the Nazis and their methods. What emerged was a philosophy so confused and incoherent that it would never have been taken seriously had it not become the official policy of a government with American support. Diem's absolute authority brought him adherents of a sort, cronies and family members whose corruption knew no limit.

In January 1963 at Ap Bac (the hamlet of Bac) on the Delta, ill-equipped guerrilla forces of the Viet Cong defeated a modern army four times its size in the first battle of the American War in Vietnam. In retrospect it is easy to call it a 'turning point', at the time it must have appeared more as a thunderbolt, hardly possible to believe. In fact it was not believed and the Americans and the South Vietnamese refused to recognize the defeat. Trinh and Tuyen were only children when this battle took place but Tuyen remembers the celebration that followed the news. They grew up to radio reports that were, of course, heavily censored. Not until they were in their teens did they begin to wonder how it happened that, in spite of great 'triumphs' on the battlefield and government declarations that the war was over, it still dragged on. The unrest in the country grew under Diem's abuse of power until it led to a series of Buddhist riots. The world was shocked by pictures of Buddhist monks burning themselves to death in protest. International disgust increased. America withdrew aid to Diem early in 1963. In

November of that year there was a military coup and Diem and his brother were assassinated. America resumed aid to the Republic and by December of 1963 there was a considerable military presence of around 16,000 troops in the country.

The Republic (RVN) that Diem created lasted for over twenty years: he ruled for nearly half that time. When Diem fell from power he left behind a state that was completely dependent on foreign (American) aid. His systematic destruction of all opposition meant that the only intact power able to succeed him was the military. Intense rivalry broke out among senior officers in the RVN jockeying for high command. High command meant power, careers and money. By far the most politically able of all the generals was Nguyen Van Thieu. He managed to survive the chaos, create his own political machine and was elected President of the RVN in 1967. Unhampered by ideology, as Diem had been, Thieu was able to integrate the political, military and economic powers. Getting rich was their common goal.

Trinh's grandfather had been ruined by Bao Dai's overthrow and her family was left with only a small piece of land in the isolated village of Mot Ngan along the Xa No River. Trinh's parents lived there with their rapidly expanding family. The marriage was a happy one and certainly fruitful – twelve children, all of whom survived childhood and, except for Trinh and her youngest sister, are still living in Vietnam. The village was one kilometer away from the provincial centre. It was not a favourable location as in between was a fairly large military installation which meant that the village was sometimes shelled, either by the Viet Cong or by incompetent RSVN soldiers. Trinh grew up to the sounds of war and intermittent shelling. Her first experience of death was when she was eight. The small school Trinh and her younger brother attended suffered a direct hit and fifteen children were killed or severely wounded. Mines strewn along the riverbank designed to keep the enemy at bay also maimed two local residents. Three times Trinh's family had to escape the advancing Viet Cong. They were fortunate enough to be able to hide on their grandfather's cargo boat and sail to Cai Rang. Cai Rang was a primarily Chinese settlement on the outskirts of Can Tho, the largest city on the southern Mekong Delta. They had a house there whereas most refugees lived on boats until the danger passed.

The Van family resources were few but Trinh's father, in proper Chinese fashion, insisted that the children be edu- cated. When they finished the local school Trinh and her brother were sent to school in Can Tho. Although the dis- tance was not great the only method of travel was by an ancient, primitive ferry boat. As the voyage of eighteen kilo- meters took over two hours, Trinh and her brother lived in Can Tho and came home only on weekends. One terrible day when she was seventeen and on her way home from school her boat was stopped. The river was blocked because of a battle somewhere near the camp. She saw smoke rising from her village and heard the familiar sounds of gunfire. Defying her elders on the boat, she jumped off and walked towards the noise. It was about three or four kilometers' dis- tance and she went slowly, always on the lookout for mines. By the time she reached the camp the fighting was over and the dead were lying on the ground in neat rows. She began to count them, then stopped, shocked at her behaviour. A small distance away were bodies of the Viet Cong scattered as they had fallen, untouched and unclaimed. Trinh made it home in a daze broken only when her father began to scold her for taking such risks. The scolding kept the hysterics at bay, at least for a while.

It was at the school in Can Tho that Trinh and Tuyen met.

14

Trinh was eleven and her brother ten when they started the new school. They spent mornings at the Vietnamese school and afternoons at a Chinese one, following a curriculum set up by the Taiwan schoolboard that included studies in Vietnamese. Trinh was the better student but Tuyen was the school hero, good at sports, handsome and the proud owner of a Honda motorcycle. When they were eighteen Trinh 'compromised' herself: she was seen riding on the back of the Honda. When the news of her indiscretion reached Mot Ngan, Trinh's mother wept: no one would marry her now, least of all Tuyen.

They were never hungry. With time the sharpness of fear dulled and sometimes years passed without trouble. Then an outburst of fighting or bombing would break the lull. From 1968 to 1971 a series of Viet Cong victories forced Trinh's family to flee once more and they spent nearly three years in Cai Rang. After 1971 they were able to move back to Mot Ngan and Trinh's two youngest siblings (numbers eleven and twelve) were born at home. Tuyen's brother, Hue, was able to buy his way out of the military. His father bribed government officials to issue new documents stating that Hue was under age for service: these made Tuyen younger still and neither of them ever served. Tuyen's brother-in-law was less fortunate. He served several years as a soldier for the South until he could stand it no longer. Then he went to a doctor who told him that with an injection he could impair the vision in one eye. The doctor swore that the damage would be temporary: it wasn't and he now has an artificial right eye. Most of his unit was wiped out in a disastrous attempt to disrupt the Ho Chi Minh trail so perhaps the bargain he made was not a bad one.

They no longer believed radio reports about the war so that when it actually ended they were all taken by surprise. Can Tho prepared itself as best it could for the conquering soldiers. Sympathisers lined the streets for hours waiting for the soldiers to arrive. Some shops were closed and some houses tightly shuttered. Their owners still believed what they read in the censored press and heard on the radio. Slowly the victors came into town: there was no triumphal parade, just groups of soldiers from the country, some from across the river, some who had been underground. When it became clear that there was nothing to fear from these joyous, exhausted men and women the whole city turned out to meet them. However, with time they began to behave like conquerors. At first their demands were simple: no long hair on young men, no tight trousers on the girls, no publicly displayed affection in couples.

The Du Cau family was a prosperous one living in Cai Rang near the South Vietnamese city of Can Tho on the fertile Mekong Delta. They had a small 'wok' factory in which both sons worked after school. Tuyen's father, who was, like most Chinese, non-political was allowed to keep the factory running. He made 'things' and 'things' were necessary to the population. At first they noticed little difference until raw material became harder and harder to come by as local resources were drained to help other, poorer, parts of the country. Trinh's family's commercial activities were outlawed although impossible to suppress. As people began to grumble about the lowered standard of living anti-Chinese feeling grew, encouraged by new restrictions. Tuyen's father was canny and had amassed enough gold to buy passage for his wife, daughter, son-in-law, and their three sons, as well as Tuyen and his older brother Hue, with their wives and children (thirteen people in all). He stayed behind for reasons that we only discovered later. John and I speculated as to why and romanticized what turned out to be un-heroic behaviour and a banal situation.

At the end of the war Vietnam experienced a form of what

is now called ethnic cleansing. The victims were the many Chinese who lived and worked there. By 1976 it had reached the very southern tip of the country where the Du Caus lived. It was a time of terrible insecurity and things seemed certain to get worse. A relative was executed for having served as an officer in the South Vietnamese army, Trinh's brother was refused entry into university and Tuyen's cousin lost his job because, although born in Vietnam, he was ethnic Chinese. The Du Caus decided it was time to leave. Their departure was semi-official as bribes had to be paid. The trick was in finding the right officials to bribe. Buses were organized (exactly by whom they never found out) and passed along the towns and villages on the Delta collecting those who had paid and whose names were on a mysterious list. Their bus contained for the most part people they knew at least by sight so they were filled with the sadness of parting, unaware of the dismay and terror that they were to know later.

When they arrived at the strip of land called Mo-O (bird's beak) on the Mekong and saw the rusty old boat twenty metres long and barely three and a half metres wide together with the crowd of terrified people waiting, they were shocked. There was, however, much worse to come. Each person was allowed to take only two changes of clothing and anything else was confiscated. They were searched for hidden gold or valuables. Once again, bribes worked and Tuyen was able by sacrificing half his money to bring part of his savings with him. Then they were herded into the hold, all 280 of them huddled together within a space that allowed practically no movement at all. For four days and nights they had no sanitation whatsoever and the fear, the swaying of the ancient boat for people who had never been to sea and the stifling heat made most of them violently sick. On the second day out a small child died and her body, wrapped in her two changes of clothing, was handed from one to another so that one of the crew could drop it overboard. Tuyen wondered that such a small package could be so heavy. Lam Ba, who was married to Tuyen's brother, Hue, was delirious to the point of not recognizing her younger son who was little more than a year old, so he was passed over to Trinh who already had four-month-old Bo. Lam Ba was so weak that she had to be carried off the boat when they finally landed. There was no food but Tuyen says that didn't matter as everyone was so sick and the surroundings so filthy that no one could eat anyway. Buckets of drinking water were sent down by one of the crew. However, the water had been collected from the Mekong before they put out to sea and it caused diarrhea and more nausea although some relief for those who could keep it down. Horrible as it was, Trinh's brother had a worse time. When he tried to leave a storm forced the boat to land on an island that belonged to Vietnam. There he was picked up by the police, taken back and thrown into prison and later sent to a re-education centre. He was kept there for over six months before he was released.

Trinh and Tuyen's skipper was so inexperienced that he landed them at first on the wrong island where armed Malaysian guards turned them away. Then they were dumped on a deserted island where they stayed for three days. What little food they had, mostly rice, came from the boat. Fortunately there were coconut palms and the shells were used as cups and plates for the rice which they boiled in sea water. Trinh said the mixture was so bitter that it took her several tries each time before she could keep it down. After three days representatives of the UN and the Red Cross came to the island and took them to the official refugee camp at Pulan Bidong where they were delivered into the hands of hostile Malaysians. The price for all this (including the necessary bribes) was approximately five thousand U.S. dollars per person, in gold, with a discount for children under ten. At Pulan Bidong they found hundreds of other refugees in varying stages of despair. The relief agencies allotted five dollars a day per person for food, which should have been sufficient. The money was, however, paid to the camp's local directors and from this the refugees received a small sack of rice, one tin of peas, one tin of sardines and one of meat each week. Each family was given a pot for cooking but nothing else. Everything, says Tuyen, was for sale. When they first arrived Trinh wanted to change her filthy clothes and was shy about changing in the open. They asked a fellow refugee if she might go into his straw shelter to change. Certainly, he said, for two dollars. Trinh changed behind a tree.

The refugees' section of Pulan Bidong was covered with makeshift shelters surrounding three semi-permanent buildings. The first two large ones housed the camp's Malaysian administrators and guards. The third was an office where forms could be filled out requesting asylum. At one time there were as many as forty thousand refugees and the one office must have seemed pitifully small to them. A representative from the American and other Consulates came once a month to sift through the papers and decide who the fortunate ones would be. Tuyen's brother-in-law had family already established in the States so they, with their three sons, were able to leave for America within a few months. For the rest of the family – 'our' three, Tuyen's brother, wife and two sons and his mother – there seemed to be nothing but extended misery. Bit by bit their material and physical reserves shrank. Trinh says they were saved because they were by the water and could at least keep clean. Tuyen tried to dig a well and, on the fifth try, luckily found drinking water.

One morning Trinh woke up to find five-month-old Bo's face was red, swollen and almost unrecognizable. It was covered with insect bites. They acted immediately. Tuyen learned that on the other side of the island Malaysian boats passed near to the shore and sold goods. His mother gave him a small piece of gold she had managed to hide. He exchanged this with the camp's guards for Malaysian money – at a wickedly fraudulent rate. He found a piece of a barrel, put it under his arm and walked over the mountain to the other side of the island. When the boat came in sight he swam out to meet it. With his Malaysian money he bought some food and a piece of nylon from the sailors. He swam and walked back with his newly acquired prize. He sold the nylon for a profit of nearly eight Malaysian dollars. With this he bought a mosquito net for Bo. The price was outrageous but Bo was safe. This became Tuyen's regular routine: walking and swimming and trading. Sometimes it was food, sometimes plastic, but without it Trinh says they wouldn't have survived. The Malaysian guards learned about this and collected their toll. Sometimes as many as five or six would waylay Tuyen, each demanding his tax: there was nothing to do but pay. Despite huge weight loss the muscles in Tuyen's legs became so developed he could no longer wear the trousers he had brought from Vietnam.

When other refugees left – for a 'third country' – they sold the thatched shelters they had been living in, but Trinh told me with justifiable pride that when they left they gave their shelter to a family with no money and four children. They were confined behind barbed wire and without the sea would have been even more desperate. Members of the Chinese colony on the island came to the edge of the fence and threw food and clothes to the refugees. Little got through this way but at least they were not totally forgotten. Trinh brought to Italy a sleazy, Susie-Wong red dress with huge yellow flowers that had been tossed over the wire by a toothless old lady who no longer had any use for it.

They had been there for over ten months when one glorious day Don Della Perugia of *Caritas* arrived on the island. A loudspeaker broadcast to the refugees that Italy had several hundred places and he would talk to anyone who wanted to go there. Many of the Vietnamese had never heard of Italy and most of the others had got their knowledge from the cinema; 'Mafia and Pizzas'. The more well-off (at this time there were still a few who hadn't been resettled) objected to the good Don, 'In Italy too many Communique'. Don della Perugia, who is a man of presence and authority, assured them that was no problem. 'We take care of that,' he promised. All the Du Caus (eight of them) were accepted. Trinh says she looked at her frail baby and burst into tears, tears of relief. It was, Trinh says, like a Vietnamese folk tale of lost children faced with the choice of two paths through the woods. They knew nothing of Europe, only that it would be different and at that stage in their lives it was certain to be better. How could she worry about the future when day to day improvisation occupied her completely? The fact that she would have to face new situations she was not prepared for by tradition or culture never entered her mind. *Caritas* obtained an attractive apartment for Tuyen's brother, Hue and his family, including his mother, in the village next to ours, so no one felt abandoned. 'Were you frightened?' I asked Trinh. Nothing frightened her, she told me, but waking every morning to see her baby getting weaker and weaker.

The Du Caus are ethnic Chinese although all, except Tuyen's mother, had been born in Vietnam. Tuyen's mother had chosen, or been chosen, to come to Vietnam. Seeking a wife, Tuyen's father went to China, found Mai, married her (she was eighteen) and brought her back to Can Tho, where she produced a daughter and two sons as well as demonstrating a remarkable head for numbers. (To see her at her abacus was a privilege.) She was a handsome woman, her looks marred only by a huge gold tooth flashing in what seemed a permanent smile. It was with considerable surprise that I learned the story of her marriage. Her husband took up with a Vietnamese woman younger than Mai by whom he had two more children. A not unfamiliar story, but with an Oriental twist. When the children (a boy and a girl) were old enough to be educated, their father took them from their Vietnamese mother and delivered them to his Chinese wife so that they could grow up as proper Chinese. I was flabbergasted at the system and even more so at the acceptance by both wives. When I met Mai I was prepared to find her meek and obedient. Obedient she had certainly shown herself to be and she seemed as passive as an unconcerned cat, but when I saw her on two different occasions defending her sons from their father I realized how foreign I was and how superficial my judgment.

The Italian experiment had proved a success for both brothers and their families. Letters went back to Vietnam regularly – slowly as the post was still primitive – filled with the wonders of The West. Tuyen's father, who I always referred to as 'The Father', decided after a year or so to come to Italy. We learned later he had been having trouble with his Vietnamese wife, which probably had something to do with his decision to come over. Perhaps it was the desire to see the rest of his family or the glorious tales of Italy that changed his mind. I'll never know exactly why – but arrive he did. When he stepped off the plane at Rome airport, all two hundred pounds, six foot two of Chinese manhood, he was greeted ecstatically by both his sons, their wives and the three grandsons. Equally enthusiastic was Mai who was more than willing to resume her duties.

Shortly after his arrival we had the entire family to dinner.

Our dining room was formerly the stables and is long and narrow, so by necessity as well as preference, we have a 'fratino' table named for those used in monastery refectories. John always sits at one end, and when we have guests, I sit at the other. That night I gave my place to The Father, partly because of language problems but mostly because I could see him only at the head of the table, any table, a position he accepted naturally. He was the kind of man who automatically became the host at whatever gathering he attended, knowing full well it was the most important position. What a handsome man he was and how unwavering were his opinions relayed to us through his family's translations. He looked like any romantic's idea of a Chinese emperor and accepted homage with practiced grace.

We had renovated the stone barn near our house for Trinh, Tuyen and Bo. The house was small but charming. Trinh sewed beautifully and Tuyen was a first-rate carpenter so they managed the lack of space with ingenuity and Oriental colour. The Father chose to move there although a room had been set aside for him at the house of Hue, the elder son. Trinh and Tuyen gave up their room to him and moved in with Bo. Soon Mai moved in, too. That was just as well as The Father required and received an enormous amount of attention. That Mai bathed him I put down to a quaint old Oriental custom but when I saw her putting on his shoes I thought it a bit much. Difficult, dictatorial, dreadful, indeed he was and I, for one, wished that he had stayed in Vietnam. And yet, one day when I saw him alone in the garden (he never did any work) looking at nothing, into nothing, I felt a terrible sorrow, stronger than I had ever felt for the others. It was, I think, being in the presence of so much loss. When it became clear just how much trouble he caused I was free to return to the enjoyment of my original dislike without a qualm. Sooner than anticipated, tensions began to rise. Trinh's face looked stretched; Tuyen was silent; I saw less and less of Mai's gold tooth. Only The Father and Bo were unaffected. We now discovered why he had stayed in Vietnam. It seems that The Father had quarrelled with his Vietnamese wife, left her and their children and taken up with yet another woman. He spoke openly about his new liaison and failed to notice, or disregarded, the family's indignation. Mai said nothing but Trinh took issue and dared to criticize The Father, a position she admits she would never have taken in Vietnam. Here she was living her new life to the full. The Father was appalled and took every opportunity to challenge Trinh.

Trinh had her own (Oriental) way of disciplining Bo. He would kneel in front of her and at her commands either pull his own hair or slap his own face. Auto-criticism begins early. I never said a word against this although it was quite an effort not to. (It was an even greater effort not to enjoy the spectacle, it was so beguiling.) The Father felt this system satisfactory only for women and took to beating Bo with a strap. Trinh, who prides herself on her modernity, was outraged and sounds of discord grew louder in a strange counterpoint like Chinese Opera without the gongs. The Father felt cheated because he hadn't gone to America and because Trinh stood up to him and was sustained by Tuyen (with what effort on his part I can only imagine). Things worsened with Trinh often in tears. Her family had been insulted, she had been called a 'horse' (the Oriental equivalent of bitch) and The Father persisted in trying Tuyen's filial loyalty. There was no back-tracking and to continue like this was intolerable. Tuyen's sister in America had opened a Chinese take-away and was doing well. She offered to take the parents but there were further problems. They were safe in Italy so refugee status papers were unattainable. A whiteish lie wouldn't hurt, I thought and it might work. So I sent them to the American Consulate here in Florence to ask for a tourist visa knowing that once in the States their daughter could apply for papers there. The consular staff had been faced with situations such as these before and the visa was denied. Virtue battled with necessity, briefly. The Father had to go. I went the very next day to the Consulate to see an acquaintance who was Vice Consul, looked her straight in the eye and lied and lied and lied. A tourist visa was arranged.

Fortunately there is a frequent turnover of Consulate personnel in Florence and my former friend was already on her way to London when the Consul General called me in a bit of a rage. I protested my innocence (lying once more) and would do it again, scolding and all.

After Mai and The Father left everyone's life changed. Bo was put in nursery school and Trinh went to work. The depth of Trinh's happiness irradiated her whole body. She had a wonderful laugh that seemed to come from deep in her lungs. She almost seemed a lung herself – so full of breath, so full of happiness. Tuyen still worked for John but when Trinh went to work they were able to save more money. They first sent Trinh's family enough to rebuild their house and set up some of her sisters in business. Later they even sent the money to build a bridge across the tributary of the Mekong where Trinh's family lived.

By 1984 the political climate in Vietnam had changed considerably and Trinh and Tuyen decided that it was safe for Trinh to go to see her family and to take six-year-old Bo with her. Although the war had been over for several years and the south had not been damaged to the extent that the north of the country had, people were still incredibly poor and living conditions primitive. Bo was frightened and too young to hide his anxiety. Nevertheless, after the first week or so the huge, loving family overcame his fears and all he missed were his tortellini and spaghetti and a proper bath-room. They were visitors from another planet in this small hamlet several hours' boat trip from the metropolis of Can Tho. People came long distances just to look at them, to gaze at their clothes, to admire Bo's toys and bombard them with questions about the outside world. The whole family became celebrities, and they seemed to spend their entire time taking photographs of each other. Trinh felt like a princess and asked if it was wrong to enjoy that. I assured her it wasn't. Since then all three have made several trips and the only limits to their travels are time and expense. By their second visit the atmosphere in Vietnam had undergone even more notable changes. The new freedom and the beginning of a modest economic recovery made life far more pleasant for them all. No need to feel guilty about our good fortune, Trinh assured me, as all my married sisters now have tele-vision.

They were blissfully young. When they came to Italy the combined ages of the three of them totalled 45. They were together, too, so adjustment came fairly quickly. When I think what they had to cope with I am filled with admira-tion: new traditions, usage, conventions, habits, religion, fashion, a completely different conception of time, new foods and above all that beastly language. Trinh was fasci-nated when I told her the story of the Tower of Babel. Oh, glorious day when the whole earth was of one language! Trinh said Jehovah was unnecessarily cruel and I agreed with her.

Although neither Trinh nor Tuyen ever left their history behind, they were soon able to add on to it their new expe-riences and to accept the habits, thoughts and behaviour of others. Trinh had always been interested and informed about the outside world when they were in Vietnam.

Although she always addressed her father in Chinese and would never have been allowed to marry a Vietnamese, most of her close friends were Vietnamese. Perhaps because his father's hold was stronger, Tuyen was more Chinese orientated – all through the war his mother had said neither she nor her sons could die as she had to go back once more to China. Both sets, of parents have indeed gone to China within the last few years, but none of the younger generations feel this pull. The idea of finding themselves in a position they considered temporary soon diminished and first Trinh and not too much later, Tuyen, realized that exile was a permanent state, not just a transitory one, and as such required new definition. Soon they were able to speak of the past with neither nostalgia nor resentment. Having a very young child growing up as an Italian and a mixture of Vietnamese, Chinese and Italian friends helped. They became Italian citizens after five years in the country and we all celebrated. We are residents of a small town outside Florence called Bagno a Ripoli and it was in the *Municipio* (City Hall) there that the ceremony of citizenship took place. The first such occasion in Bagno and of great importance to everyone, curiosity mixed with tenderness. The law required four witnesses (John and I were not eligible as we are not Italian citizens) but there was no shortage. Between friends and colleagues there were twelve. The ceremony was simple and happily brief, the spumante flowed and the Mayor gave Trinh her first congratulatory kiss.

PART II

'What I am is not important, whether I live or die –
    It is the same for me, the same for you.
What we do is important. This is what I have learnt.
    It is not what we are but what we do,'

Says a child in exile, one of a family
    Once happy in its size. Now there are four
Students of calamity, graduates of famine,
    Those whom geography condemns to war,

Who have settled here perforce in a strange country,
    Who are not even certain where they are.
They have learnt much. There is much more to learn.
    Each heart bears a diploma like a scar –

PHNOM PENH HAD fallen to the Khmer Rouge before Saigon but there was little or no news from there. When the news did come out it was so horrific, so devastating it was difficult at first to believe. We felt more helpless than ever.

Once again we turned to James for counsel and assistance. He had spent a great deal of time in Cambodia, especially during the 'Decent Interval' between the Paris Agreement of 1973, which ended direct American participation in the war, and the final victory of the Khmer Rouge in 1975. He had made many friends there and it was through one of them that we, in a roundabout way, made contact with our Cambodian family.

After the Du Caus had been with us for almost a year James came to visit. He had just returned from a trip to a Thai/Cambodian frontier refugee camp to find a friend who had worked for him in Phnom Penh. His experience was similar though less dramatic than that of Sidney Schanberg, the journalist whose story was filmed in *The Killing Fields*. In the camp he was besieged by refugees begging his help in getting them to a 'third country'. Among them was a twelve- or thirteen-year-old Cambodian orphan boy who made a great impression on him. This boy was teaching himself English and his cleverness and charm delighted James. James sent him some English text books and promised to do what he could for him. Because of the experience with Binh, and seeing how well the Du Caus had adapted to Tuscan life, he thought of us. James felt that here was a boy capable of learning another language and absorbing another culture, someone who would profit from exposure to the West.

As he talked John and I kept looking at each other and long before James had finished his story John was nodding his head. We were sitting around the swimming pool where two-year-old Bo and his four- and six-year-old cousins, Peng and Ang, were splashing. The deliciousness of those babies made me happy and, in a strange way, eager to take on more responsibility, and more love. We talked it over and decided that we could probably afford to take on another child. It was a big step, and we spent many hours discussing it with James.

But what were we going to do? There was no Don Luigi, no *Caritas*. I remembered that the Italian Ambassador to Thailand was a friend of friends so I wrote asking his advice and if possible his help. He was, as to be expected, extremely polite. Repeated letters and telexes to the Embassy in Bangkok brought an invitation to dinner but not much in the way of information. There seemed little that they could do as all I had was the boy's name (Samreth Soarith Khul) and a tracing number at the Children's Center 8, Khao-I-Dang Refugee Camp. With only this information they were unable to contact the lad. A profound contempt for bureaucracy and considerable arrogance led me to believe I could do better on the spot, so I decided to fly to Thailand and 'fight City Hall' from there. I was determined to do everything possible to keep bureaucracy from destroying another child. I first stopped in London, to consult with James.

Over a sumptuous tea at Brown's Hotel in London I received instructions and information from James together with bookings he had arranged for me. His advice was complicated but invaluable. It included a list of offices where permission to visit the camp could be obtained and various instructions: 'Go to Joint Operation Centre; Supreme

Command; Ministry of Defense' and a mysterious note in James's handwriting: 'Task Force 80' (neither of us remember what it or he meant). I needed to obtain, according to James, a pink card to enter the camp. I ended up, after three irritating days in Bangkok, with a white printed form from the Ministry of Defense written in Thai. I took this document to the Supreme Command. The official there, in impeccably starched khakis, asked me if I remembered Deanna Durbin and wrote four short lines in graceful Thai script at the bottom. He then took it into his superior for signature (in pencil) and a stamp that didn't want to stick. Strange how comforting a cyclostyled piece of paper can be. I felt armed, protected, invulnerable and went away hoping to be challenged so that I might wave my miraculous paper in the air. Still following James's instructions, I went to the Trocadero Hotel to look up the concierge, Rocky (not his real name he told me) who, according to James, knew everyone and arranged everything. The Trocadero looked wicked in a Hollywood way – not old or attractive enough for Graham Greene decadence – and was where most of the visiting journalists stayed.

James had made reservations for me at the Inter-Continental hotel for what he said was my comfort and I was grateful. Rocky engaged a Thai taxi, and negotiated what seemed to me a very reasonable price, for the fourth day of my stay (Friday) when I planned to go to the camps. I slept little Thursday night and was up shortly before five in the morning for my six o'clock appointment in front of the Siam Inter Continental. The driver was also eager and I found him waiting for me at twenty to six with the car's air conditioning already functioning. It was November and very hot. Bangkok at that hour of the morning was happily free of traffic jams but not a bit more attractive. Water was still standing in spots where the drains had backed up, garbage had not been collected for days, the fetid air was heavy with the smell of spoiled fruit and flowers, corpses of mongrel dogs were left alongside the road (I counted three that day).

It was, the Thai taxi driver assured me, a pleasant four-hour drive from Bangkok to the Refugee Camp at the Cambodian border. Except for a stop for petrol and a cool drink (beer for me and an orange drink of dubious colour for him) we had been on the road for nearly six hours before we sighted anything. More than once I thought myself mad to have made the trip at all but never once during that long dreary day did I think of turning back. Driving out of Bangkok into the countryside calmed me down. The paddy fields glowed with a green I had never seen before, ever changing yet repeating itself. The driver's card, which he showed but didn't give me (I suspect he only had one), advertised him as 'a English speeker'. He seemed pleased to have someone to practice on and chattered away, which was comforting, like rather discreet movie music. Fields and villages disappeared; a reddish-grey dust was everywhere and the newly laid asphalt was covered with it. I had been on the lookout for the hills that marked the Cambodian border and the end of the camp but the dust and the heat-haze hid them until we had almost arrived. I was thinking vertically, of hills, but what struck me was surrealy horizontal. If it is true (as I read somewhere) that the imagination pictures objects vertically and reality pictures them horizontally, this was 'reality' to drown in. The buildings (low thatched huts) seemed to cover the land without end. There were, I learned from one of the aid workers, 120,000 people housed there, down from a previous high of 150,000.

The pass that I had spent three days obtaining from the Thai authorities did not include the driver so I left him at the camp's entrance. He locked himself in the car, stretched out and waved me off happily.

34

I wonder if the aid worker was as sublimely wonderful as he remains in my memory. An Italian-American named Tom Generico, he had been working at the camp for more than two years. His rapport with the Cambodian refugees seemed to me just right: a humorous, concerned authority. He teased and was teased by the young and was fatherly to the tiny peasant woman who came into his office in tears; he was as proud of his halting Cambodian as his interpreters were of their English. Once arrived at Khao-I-Dang I willingly put myself in Tom's hands. He showed me around the office and then took me to the Children's Center 8 with its rows of bunk beds and photographs covering all available wall space. When a refugee arrived in camp his photograph was taken and circulated in the hope that the new arrival would be recognized, if not by family members or friends, at least by someone from his village. Families were often reunited that way. He found Samreth's picture for me and the sight of a bewildered young boy holding tightly on to a placard with his name (incorrectly spelled) written in large block letters made me more determined than ever to find him. There was nothing of childish sadness in that face, only the gloom of adult grief: grave and mute. The sight of all those photos, and an occasional blank space to denote success, filled me with an almost personal grievance.

Samreth had been helping some of the volunteer doctors and had gone with them to another, smaller camp fairly nearby. So, after thanking Tom and his Cambodian assistants, the driver and I took off for the second camp, Panat Nikhom Holding Centre, Chonburi. It was run by a young woman, Churu Naktipwan. She was pretty in that small-boned Thai way and spoke French and passable English. She told me that Samreth's photograph had been recognized by his mother and he had been sent to a third camp to meet her. I got back into the taxi for the third camp, which was smaller still, but full of activity. We arrived just as huge sacks of rice were being distributed. I found this suffocatingly depressing. Perhaps it was the permanence that those huge sacks implied. Perhaps, coming from the world of the rich, it was seeing the desires and needs of the destitute. Worse still was the news that Samreth and his mother were on their way back to Khao-I-Dang. It was then almost dark so a further trip would have been dangerous and we wouldn't have been admitted. There was nothing for it but to return to Bangkok.

Back in the car I began to cry. I felt a fool crying in the back of a Thai taxi. I cried as softly as possible trying not to disturb my friend, the driver. He offered to do anything, drive through the night, break down the gates, anything: but we went back.

I somehow managed to get through the visits and calls to various Embassies, Relief Agencies and Government Offices in Bangkok that followed, though I remember little about the remaining days. People were generally pleasant and promises were made but at that stage I felt little hope. The day before my flight home I collapsed at a shopping centre near my hotel. The souvenir-shop owner seeing my distress brought out a chair and a glass of water and after sitting with my head down and being cooed over by some children, I made it back to my room. I called the hotel doctor. I was in a fog, confused and anything but pleased when he congratulated me on my new president – until then I had satisfactorily avoided thinking about the American election and the victory of Ronald Reagan. When the doctor could find nothing wrong and learned that I had been to the camps he prescribed Valium, and it worked like a charm. Still in a daze from all the wretchedness I had seen, as well as the Valium, I flew back home.

All the written messages to Samreth had gone through, thanks to Tom. A letter arrived in Florence shortly after my return. It was written in the name of Samreth's mother, Sou Sary, and said: 'I thank your letter sent to me on Nov 20, 1980 and said that you will help me and my family for living in Italian in the future. Myself and my family are very happy to wait for that.' Then she, or the person who wrote the letter for her went on to say, 'I am informing you that since my arrival in Khao-I-Dang I have quiet often got the sadest news on Kampuchea and about the Khmer people in general who have been suffered from the Vietnames.' I learned later that Sary considered the Vietnamese her saviours and had not understood the words of her scribe. The arrival of the Vietnamese had made escape possible (nor would she have said 'Kampuchea', a Khmer Rouge name). Ironically many of those who escaped with her were from the ranks of her tormentors. The letter continued, 'It is quite obvious to me that the separation of relatives and blooded people as well as the lose of all properties and previous belonging make the whole Khmer meet with their endless sorrows. I am earnestly hopeful, I shall be receipt of your reply in the short time.' Then she told us that her family consisted of herself, Samreth and his younger sister, Kilen. John and I were surprised but pleased. I rang Don Luigi with the news. He asked if I thought the girl really was a sister: I answered 'Chi se ne frega' (politely translated as 'Who gives a damn?') 'Ben detto' said Don Luigi, emphatically.

At that stage matters seemed more urgent than ever so I, having lived in Italy for more than twenty years, resorted to a local custom called *raccomandazione* (literally the word means recommended, actually it means pulling strings). I rang a friend in Milan, a Socialist Senator, and explained the problem. He 'recommended' me to ring the private telephone number of a functionary he knew at the *Ministero degli Estero* (Foreign Ministry). Within a week we received telex confirmation from the Italian Embassy in Bangkok. Approval had been granted for Samreth, mother and sister to come to Italy and as soon as the necessary medical examinations had been done, they would be on their way.

'Abbia pazienza' (Be patient, a necessary and useful Italian phrase) said the functionary when I rang his secret number after a two-month silence. I tried. Then, three days later on Monday 16 February, John received a phone call in his office; it was the efficient functionary. His message: Thursday 19 February, 1981, at six o'clock in the morning the Khul family arrives at the Roman airport of Fiumicino. He went further: the family consisted of Sou Sary (the mother), Samreth, the sister Kilen and the *piccolo bambino*. John was no longer surprised – he was in shock! 'Where did he come from?' he wanted to know. 'That is what we were wondering, too' was the answer. 'How old is the *piccolo bambino*?' John asked thinking he might be an indiscretion of the camp. He was, as near as could be figured out, eight years old. John and I speculated: was he really a brother? Did it matter if he wasn't? How was he found? None of our speculations came anywhere near the actual facts as we were later to learn them.

On the Wednesday we drove to Rome and spent the night in a hotel near the airport. Neither of us slept. I had a noisy, churning stomach and John couldn't stop talking. We rose early and rushed through an icy rain to the airport. The Air Thai plane had come in seventy minutes ahead of schedule, and the Roman officials were still shaking their heads in wonder when we arrived. There was no one left in the arrival lounge but two Carabinieri and the Khuls. The first thing that struck me was their beauty; Sary, Samreth and Kilen; the delicacy and the beauty. Hiding behind Samreth's back was the '*piccolo bambino*' but when I put out my hand he came forward and took it trustingly. Kilen and her mother were wearing cotton sarongs and T-shirts, the boys shorts and T-shirts. All wore plastic flip-flops without socks. Samreth was carrying a minute duffel bag that seemed to hold the family's entire possessions. They came towards me with the Buddhist gesture of clasped hands and bowed head but when I kissed each one they seemed neither frightened nor dismayed. Samreth spoke some English and Sary some French so welcome was made clear.

In Italy jokes – the Irish or Polish variety – are made about the Carabinieri and the two that morning might well have qualified. They were, luckily for us, wonderfully humane. They saw my anxiety, the shivering Cambodians and the deserted lounge. Taking it all in, especially the latter, they let us leave without any of the dreaded formalities, which included, we had been told, the possibility of a temporary quarantine. I signed a large register and took consignment of the family, as though it was a cumbersome but possibly valuable package. Never had I so blessed an organizational muddle. We rushed out of the airport (I didn't want to risk seeing any other officials) to find John waiting at the exit with the motor running and the car heater blazing.

Houssara, the *piccolo bambino*, sat in front with John and myself, the others in the back. I mostly noticed how softly they chattered, how beautifully they smiled. Most of the conversation was carried on through Samreth, the English speaker of the family, although it was clear that he deferred to his mother. John had said to me before they arrived, 'Would it be too much to ask if the girl was pretty?' He was dazzled by Kilen's loveliness, Sary's dignified beauty and Samreth's romantic head. Houssara was an instantly lovable, agile, grinning imp. The three-hour drive to Florence seemed interminable, it was as though the world had stopped. It reminded me of my first transatlantic flight. I now felt that the entire world was encapsulated in our old Alfa

Romeo. Children are naturally more aware of the future than adults. We are forever worrying about the present or regretting the past. That day I felt positively childlike. Never have I felt so willing to be defined, influenced or even determined by what was to happen next.

John had thought that music would ease the tension and put *The Nutcracker* on the car tape recorder. It was an astute idea, lifting the atmosphere and distracting us all. The Goldberg Variations would have been an even better choice but how were we to know that this soon. We stopped at one of the Autostrada restaurants but no one had any appetite. On our way out we passed a glass case inside which was a gimcrack toy automobile. Houssara stopped and put his hand, palm up, on the glass to get as close as possible to the wondrous object. John bought the car for him and he squealed with surprise. His expectancy level was very low. Even after he had been with us for a while he was always amazed by any gift no matter how small. The anticipation of pleasure was missing to such a degree that he never seemed unhappy when he didn't get a gift, unusual in any child, incredibly rare in an eight-year-old. On the other hand a gift, no matter how welcome, was never thought of as a bribe as it often is with young children. Pleasure was so unexpected it was greeted with wonder and unequivocal delight. Houssara had never had the chance to learn the rights and wishes of a child. Samreth tried to tell John it hadn't been necessary to buy the car but Sary, who was wiser, hushed him. Back in the car Houssara fell asleep clutching his car. He slept until John stopped the car by the roadside, needing a pee. By then it had begun to snow. None of the Cambodians had ever seen snow but at least the older ones had heard or read about it. To Houssara it was a complete revelation and he scrambled out of the car, lifted his face to the sky and laughed and laughed.

We left the Autostrada at Firenze Sud and took the back road for home. As we neared our house on the steep, winding road with its terraced olive groves which to us is so beautiful, conversation ceased and smiles became forced and infrequent. Only Houssara seemed unaffected. Something was obviously wrong but we didn't find out until later that 'hills' meant danger: bandits, tigers, unmentionable terror. We had much to learn. Nor had we thought about the age-old enmity between the Vietnamese and the Cambodians. I thought shyness was the reason for the rather cool reception given and received by the two families when we introduced them. That first night when Tuyen picked up a sleeping Houssara and carried him to bed I was startled to see Sary stiffen. Wrapped in our own familiar neuroses and prejudices, we are apt to dismiss those of others without proper consideration. There is an old Cambodian proverb the children loved to repeat that translates roughly: The Chinese will never lose his shrewdness; the Vietnamese will never lose his wickedness and the Cambodian will never lose his sexiness.

That first night after everyone was in bed and the house was quiet, John and I opened a bottle of cold Vernaccia and took it into our bedroom. We were so tired, too tired even to drink the wine in our glasses. We lay in bed scarcely able to move, with nothing fitting to say to one another, only a numb happiness. To try and talk about it would have seemed wrong: we lay back and shared the sudden sense of quiet and rest and relief.

The first days passed rapidly, as excitement quickly gave way to exhaustion. We were in the middle of a fierce winter: any winter would have been fierce for the Cambodians, but 1981 was record-breaking. Sleep and warm clothing were the priorities for everyone. A look into Samreth's duffel bag revealed two extra sarongs, two pairs of shorts and three T-shirts, plus a Bible translated into Cambodian (a gift of the Camp's Missionaries), a pestle with a crudely hollowed-out wooden mortar and a string of garlic. Telephone calls to friends brought an avalanche of warm clothing, most of it very chic. My bedroom became a cross between a bazaar and a boutique, and there was great giggling as clothes were tried on and accepted or discarded. Everyone except Houssara had very definite ideas as to what suited. Style gave way to comfort for Kilen who put on two skirts, two sweaters and four pairs of socks before she snuggled into a lined wind-breaker. Sary managed to look elegant in an oversized woolen dress that she draped like a sarong and Samreth rigged himself up as a stylish cross country skier. Only Houssara didn't seem to feel the cold or care what was put on him.

To begin with only Samreth went out of the house. No one else wanted to leave. Sary was too depressed; Kilen too obsessed with food, spending most of her time in the kitchen, cooking, eating or looking lovingly at the pantry shelves, arranging and re-arranging fruits and vegetables until she created a still life worthy of a Dutch painting. They had all been adequately fed in the camp although the diet seemed to consist of rice, beans, tinned sardines and Spam. The tins were wonderful they said, their only objection was to the over-abundance of beans. Kilen soon became plump, too plump for her tiny frame. I could not, and would not, discourage her from eating – it was so important to her. Many years later she told me that her mother kept saying she must save food for her older brother, she must eat less as there were four of them and she feared we would not keep them if they ate too much. I will never know if this was meant seriously or was a mother's strategy to make Kilen lose weight. Kilen still believes it was the former and Sary no longer remembers. At the time Kilen was convinced that in a former life she had been ungenerous with a Buddhist monk's begging bowl and this was her punishment. She seemed resigned to put on weight until she burst.

Each boy had a room to himself and Sary and Kilen shared a twin bedroom (I always found them in the same small bed those first days). Samreth had Lisa's old room (she had moved into her own house a few years before) and Houssara had the room at the very top of what was once a watchtower. We reckoned that the extra flight of stairs wouldn't bother him. What we hadn't reckoned with was the terror of finding himself alone. The youngest of a large family, from a society where generations still live together, herded by the Khmer Rouge into a camp at five, he had never spent a night alone. He stood at the foot of each flight of stairs leading to his room (there were four), paused, looked around carefully and muttered incantations before ascending. With each flight of steps the pauses grew longer, the incantations louder until at the foot of the final stairs his voice could be heard distinctly rooms away. The words themselves made no sense even to Samreth who, seeing his fear, offered to accompany him. The offer was firmly, heroically, refused.

Music was a big help. John had ordered two series of records made by UNESCO, one of Cambodian and one of Vietnamese traditional music. We were very proud of ourselves when we presented these. Everyone listened politely, probably trying as hard as I was to find them fascinating, and then Trinh asked if we had *West Side Story* and Kilen and Samreth began singing Khmer Rouge songs. The greatest success was a record known as 'Bo's music' – a recording of medieval music from the court at, of all places, Prague. For some reason, perhaps the drum and cymbals and simple rhythms of these brief, lively pieces caught everyone's fancy and soon we were all dancing with the indefatigable Bo.

As every foreign resident in Italy knows an office of fundamental importance is *L'Ufficio per Stranieri* at the *Questura* (the office for foreigners of the civilian police). It is here that all foreigners wanting to live in Italy must register, within ten days of arrival. If accepted the newcomer is issued with a *Permesso di Soggiorno* valid from one to four years depending on official assessment of the applicant's potential. Until recently many people, including myself, ignored the law but the document has now become a necessity. No bank account can be opened, no automobile purchased, no work permit obtained, no official document signed without exhibiting a *Permesso di Soggiorno*. Armed with as many documents as possible I took Samreth and Sary with me to fill out the forms for the *Soggiorno* and to request the Geneva Convention passports to which they were entitled as stateless persons and political refugees. The Florentine *Questura* in February 1981 was chaotic, but I was perfectly at home there as I had done the paperwork for Trinh and Tuyen, and after several fruitless visits, in true Italian style, I had made a friend. The Dottoressa Giovanna Nocera was slight, very southern, and so nearsighted she held all papers within inches of her pebble-thick lenses, tilting her head in her effort to sneak up on the words. She was intelligent, determined and wished us all well. She ran her department with iron-handed efficiency. I wonder how many frightened refugees (political and economic) owe their relative well-being to the Dottoressa Giovanna. I happened into the *Questura* the day before she retired and there was gloom and confusion everywhere. Her particular responsibilities had been divided into three sections, each section with its own head. The new Dottoresse were all younger, better dressed and in full possession of their faculties, yet they inspired little confidence either in me or in their fellow workers.

When Giovanna had finished the mound of documents for Sary and Samreth, we were ushered into the office of the *Maresciallo*, head of the local police, to be signed up once more. Large, greying and rather handsome, the *Maresciallo* wore his authority with a certain ease. He sat me down in a fake-leather chair in front of his large, empty desk and motioned to Sary and Samreth to take straight-back chairs slightly behind me. Since we had little to say to one another, Dottoressa Giovanna having done all the work, he struck up a conversation about world affairs. His knowledge was limited but not his indignation which was wide and fierce. I am a past master at the exchange of banalities and since the *Maresciallo* needed to pass a certain amount of time before lunch we went at it seriously. At one moment he railed against the Khmer Rouge with such vehemence I turned around to take in Sary and Samreth and let them enjoy his condemnation. I was stunned to see them clutching each other in abject terror. They hadn't understood a word of the conversation and the violence of this powerful man plus the mere mention of the Khmer Rouge had terrified them both. I apologized profusely and the *Maresciallo* patted their hands and hugged Samreth for reassurance. I cursed myself for my insensitivity and ignorance.

Looking at Sary it was difficult to believe what had happened to her. Physically she seemed unmarred: she had the slimness of a girl as well as clear eyes and glowing, golden skin. She walked with out-turned feet in the manner of Oriental women, her back was straight but not stiff and she had the diplomat's gift of well timed silences. She was a beautiful woman which made the sorrow in her eyes more poignant still. She did her best to be jolly but sometimes, when the children were at school, I would find her sitting in the corner of the kitchen in a straight-back chair (she always did this when she was particularly depressed). She seemed to welcome company, so that when I could I sat with her, speaking little. The air was thick with despair, mottled with grief. When she did speak it was always the same: she would look around her in disbelief, shake her head and say, 'Where are they, where are my tall brothers?'

Of the three children, Samreth looked the most like his mother. In a strange way, Samreth's head seemed too substantial and important for his body. It was a wonderful head, the skin pulled tautly over high cheekbones, a nose that was almost aquiline, large sensuous lips and a dreamy far away look in his eyes as though he was searching for a setting star. He had a long, deep dimple on his left cheek and, thank heavens, crooked teeth that marred the perfection. He had enormous, immediate and continuous success with girls – and with their mothers, too.

Kilen was lovely although she did her best to disguise it. She could not hide her smile, her grace and when she spoke, her voice. One always felt she pulled back even when standing still and it took several months before she could accept a compliment without running from the room. She was neat, almost prim, and her clothes were always a size too large. She admired her friends, the girls in her class at school but she never dared to imitate their style. Her timidity slowly lessened, she once embraced me out of genuine feeling and then seeing what she had done pretended to give me a massage to conceal her impulsiveness. After about a year the embraces were no longer tentative and embarrassing to her and she began to hug John with almost the same force. We had always held large, boisterous birthday parties for Simon and Lisa and it was a tradition I wanted to continue with the children. Houssara was delighted with the idea, Samreth accepted graciously but sceptically, Kilen refused. She was still not comfortable being the centre of attention.

Houssara was an immediate success with everyone who

came to the house and at school as well. There were no out-
ward signs of suffering on this sturdy, well-built eight-year-
old with the mischievous, practically permanent grin. There
is an Italian word *birichino* that describes him well: lively,
shrewd, slightly naughty and irresistible. One friend suggested a great future for him organizing the Cambodian
Mafia – how very little she understood! His mind never
stopped turning over ideas, even at eight or nine. He was
unstinting with his affections which he gave with a spon-
taneity that not everyone understood. Those that did (and
still do), treasure the affection, those that misread him have
wounded him, sometimes severely. For a child so young he
had quite an accurate picture of the strength and weakness
of others but not always of his own. His sense of humour
was sometimes over-charged. He knew when to stop,
instinctively, but was tempted at times to keep on going. He
often played practical jokes: the pleasure of deception without serious intent or malice delighted him. He did, however,
save his harshest jokes for those in whom he felt a lack of
authentic feeling. He once told me that since he knew who
he was and what he wanted, he found it odd that this wasn't
easily recognizable to others. His ideas and feelings were
subject to change but never ungenuine at the time.

One of his earliest attachments (a friendship so deep that
most adults preferred to ignore it) was with a girl his age
who lived near us. They were in the same class at school and
inseparable after school. For two years they saw one another
daily, automatically. Then the girl moved away with her
parents and went to another school. She cried for weeks
before the move and his face was grey with disappointment.
They exchanged visits, sometimes sleeping over at each
other's house until she suddenly began to bloom as young
girls do and outgrew him. Now they are once again friends.
I have realized, only recently, that he never considered

himself a child, even as an eight-year-old. A friend's four-year-old daughter came to visit last year when Houssara was twenty-one. Her mother had supplied her with distractions to relieve the boredom of adult company. She took out her large colouring book and Houssara was fascinated as he had never seen one before – he had skipped that part of his life.

He was unbelievably generous with his new possessions. We had bought him an electric train, at first just a modest few cars and tracks, then a great friend added on to it a splendid series of bridges, towns, tracks and cars until the set was extraordinary. The whole set was so large we built a waist-high wooden platform with a hole in the middle for Houssara to stand in and control the lot. Another friend bought him a railroad worker's cap for authenticity: Houssara thanked him but refused to wear it – he told me later that it made the whole thing look like a game. It was most impressive. His school friends came to admire it and Houssara demonstrated with great dignity but always gave way to the others and allowed them to become chief engineers. We often went, in those days, to a small, Italian speaking town near the Istrian coast, and we usually took the children with us. Houssara made a friend at once, a boy a year younger named Samuele. They became such friends that Houssara asked if he might give Samuele his train set as Samuele's family now had electricity in their house and they were far too poor ever to buy him such a magnificent gift. On the following trip we arrived with the entire set boxed carefully by Houssara and Samreth (who thought his brother mad). The excitement and pleasure when we drove to Samuele's house was intense – both theirs and ours.

Shortly after their arrival we had a visit from James who wanted to see how Samreth was settling in and to meet the rest of the family. We were joined by James's sister, Elizabeth, a great favourite with them all, especially

Houssara, who admitted, years later, that she had been his first love. James took Samreth to Pisa for the day. They climbed the Leaning Tower, which frightened Samreth – he saw it as the work of a malign force. The trip was, however, a success as it emphasized Samreth's special position as first born and allowed him to feel he had a 'home' to return to after an exciting day out. Then Elizabeth had an inspired idea. She and James took the entire family on the train to Pistoia (a half-hour train ride, but their first) and a visit to the zoo with lunch, Houssara told me, at the 'best' restaurant he had ever been to. (It was also his first!)

Not all 'treats' were so successful. Lisa, who lives close by, and a friend, decided to take all three children camping at the sea. Elaborate preparations were made, a luxurious tent was bought together with the latest cooking equipment, a new roof-rack was put on the car with a great deal of difficulty. Everyone but Houssara hated the trip. The idea that sleeping in a tent could be fun never entered their minds. Kilen refused to go into the sun as she didn't want to get darker and sat huddled in the tent the entire time while Samreth built complicated figures in the sand. Houssara and Lisa were the only ones in the water. The new cooking equipment was not even unwrapped: the only thing they enjoyed was the pizzeria and trattoria food at night – the picnic during the day was too reminiscent of past meals in the paddy. They cut the 'vacation' short and Lisa said they only began to laugh and chatter as they neared home. 'I loved camping at their age' said Lisa, forgetting that she had always lived in a comfortable house. She and her friend said they felt rather like a divorced couple who had undertaken a holiday together for the children's sake – everyone trying to put a brave face on what was obviously not a success. Even pizzas and ice cream and forced jollity could not mask the fact that the whole thing had been a dreary mistake.

49

I remarked to James, who had spent quite a bit of time in Cambodia and who knew the language, on what seemed to me a lack of maternal attention in Sary, especially towards Houssara, the youngest. He explained that it was the responsibility of the older children in a family to care for and discipline their younger siblings. Having been brought up in a large family herself, Sary realized the importance of each child having a distinct place within the family group. Both Kilen and Samreth were zealous in doing their duty when it came to discipline. Sary told me years later that when a child was born it was handed straight over to the nurse. She had done her part; she had produced the child and its daily care would now be the duty of others. It was clearly tradition and custom, not lack of love. Sary would sometimes gaze at them all with such amazement and scared, swift love that it was painful to watch and I would be forced to look away.

I believe that parents should, whenever possible, explain things to a child – it was something I had always tried to do with my own children. How was I to manage now? The children had to learn, but their mother was present as part of our 'family'. It was a difficult path to tread for everybody, requiring more tact than I would normally use. For the first weeks at least language would be an insurmountable obstacle, and then there were cultural differences to tackle as well. And yet there had to be some rules. Kilen gave me an early opportunity to explain, wordlessly and, I hope, painlessly. The issue was unimportant, a can of dogfood that she felt was too good for an animal and which she proceeded to eat to show me. There were lessons to be had for both of us. I learned that children can be satisfied with an explanation that they can't possibly understand and that a firm 'no' means just that, even though it seems to make no sense at all. At the very least the child learns that what he wants to know is difficult to understand, which is in itself a kind of self-knowledge. She learned, I found out later, that I could be humoured without enormous effort on her part. I liked being humoured by Kilen and her rare compliments grew to mean a great deal to me. She and I had the most turbulent relationship of all. Only after a while could we pass time together without serious misunderstanding which usually ended in rows or, if we were lucky, laughter. One day there was a confusion about collecting her from a friend's house. I made two trips of several kilometres each as she wasn't at the spot where she was supposed to meet me. When I finally collected her I was cross, very, and gave her a severe talking-to. She put her head down and her shoulders began to shake. 'Now, don't cry,' I said, afraid I had gone too far. 'I'm not, I'm not,' she said and I could see then that she was doubled up with laughter, I looked so funny when I was furious. We were both laughing so hard I had to stop the car. 'You see,' she told me, 'you have become much more mature.' I thanked her and we both agreed that maturity was something hilarious.

On the language front, we arranged for a local secondary school teacher named Roberta to come to the house daily to give Italian lessons to all four. We also tried to teach them as much as we could ourselves. It was an unusual situation as we were teaching them to speak Italian which was not our own first language. Each had his own method of dealing with the new knowledge. An old friend of ours, Luigino Franchetti, himself an accomplished linguist, said Italian was the simplest language to 'speak at', in other words, it is relatively easy to make oneself understood in Italian but it is one of the most difficult languages to speak perfectly. My knowledge of other languages is limited but I do not doubt him. Both of our children speak Italian as a first language and John is almost as perfect. I, alas, have little ear and although fluent, my Italian is far, far from correct. I warned Kilen not to use me as an example but she had already worked out that for herself.

Sary, I was to learn, had lived in government circles and accepted instruction graciously and smiled a great deal. Samreth charmed Roberta and soon became 'teacher's pet'. He was the first to try speaking Italian. Strangely for some-one so musical he had little 'ear' for language. Perhaps say-ing he had little interest is more accurate. For such an emotional boy he was extremely practical about words: he quickly learned the necessary ones and their basic applica-tion. Using these, with little concern for sequence and none for grammar, he soon made himself understood. After an impressive start his spoken or written Italian scarcely improved. Within a year or so he began to write poetry in Italian, some of which I still have. His poems consist of unconnected, disturbing images and intensely personal moments that would fascinate any analyst. What got him through school was his extraordinary visual memory as he was able to memorize whole pages from his text books.

Kilen, the only one who had an interest, even a passion, for language, listened intently and her lips moved as she fol-lowed everything Roberta said. I heard her afterwards repeating the day's lesson, chirping away in a near perfect imitation of Roberta. Kilen was, like the birds, never off-key, her voice was unmusical only when she was frightened. She was a fantastic mimic, curing me of two behavioural 'tics' of which I had been unaware until I recognized them in her imitations.

Houssara was completely indifferent to the lessons although he sat quietly at Samreth's orders, like a well-behaved puppy. He showed no noticeable progress until John made him a series of cards with Italian words printed on them, which he used to construct airplanes or houses.

When he made an airplane out of a full sentence John felt rewarded. Since he was so young John and I thought he would have very little trouble with the language. We were wrong but for unusual and very personal reasons. From the time he could speak at all he wanted to have what he later called philosophical discussions. Even at ten 'The Meaning of Life' interested him more than soccer. He wanted to talk about those things inside himself, his thoughts and feelings, long before he had a suitable vocabulary. His mind was quick and genuinely curious, his conversations often difficult, if not impossible, to follow. I once asked him the name of a familiar object, I don't remember exactly what but it was something as simple as 'chair' and he didn't know the word for it. When I asked why he said, 'If it's outside of me I can show it to you, can't I?' He nurtured his ideas, clung to them and fought for them the way most children fight for toys. The ideas themselves were often extravagant, even absurd – something he never admitted but must have sensed as he began to discard the more exotic ones.

Our knowledge about Cambodia came from news reports, a book by Norman Lewis, *A Dragon Apparent*, and conversations with James. We were, quite naturally, curious and eager for more information, especially about the children. Samreth would shake his head and mutter 'terrible, terrible' and not much more. I could not bring myself to question Sary. Kilen was silent, too, until the feast of San Giovanni. John the Baptist is the patron saint of Florence and his feast day on 24 June calls for a large and noisy celebration. Although we live in the country it is only thirteen kilometres to the Duomo and sound travels, especially the sound of an elaborate firework display. John was away on business and Lisa and I were sipping wine and chatting in my bedroom at the head of the first flight of stairs when we heard a bloodcurdling shriek. We rushed upstairs to find Kilen in near hysterics and Sary and Samreth sitting on the stairs clutching each other. From this distance the fireworks sounded for all the world like a serious bombardment. Houssara did not wake up at all. When we had explained and calmed everyone down, Kilen began to talk. All the words that had been dammed up inside her came rushing out. It was like Phnom Penh she said. The beginning of all the years of horror were the bombardments. For a few moments she felt she was no longer safe, would never be safe, that the terror was starting all over again. She talked and talked until her tears choked her. She told us of her older sister, Poutherein, who they had lost contact with but hoped was still alive. Samreth folded himself into himself like a lotus blossom at sundown and Sary sat pale and silent throughout. This was somehow the beginning of our sharing, in a very limited way, their experiences.

Samreth, too, began to open up and talk about his past. One day he came home from school in dismay. Some of his friends had asked him about Cambodia and he had told them a few stories. After a bit it was clear to him that, although no one said so, they did not believe him. 'And I did not even tell them the really terrible things,' he said.

Even Sary began to talk about the past. For the most part about her losses, her husband, her children, her parents and her brothers. Sary was the eldest of seven, after her were three beloved brothers. They all perished. The oldest was an engineer and was forced by the Khmer Rouge to supervise the digging of an irrigation canal and was then killed in the wholesale slaughter of the 'intellectuals' that followed. The second had been a supporter of Pol Pot and had secretly supplied him and his troops with money and ammunition. When he learned the truth about Khmer Rouge brutality he starved himself to death. She never learned how the third – she assured me the most beautiful of all – died. In Khao-I-Dang she met his wife's parents who had somehow survived. They told her what little they knew. His name had been called by the Khmer Rouge, together with their daughter and the couple's child. They all three disappeared. A week or so later they saw one of the Khmer Rouge cadres distributing their clothes to some of the workers. They could only assume the worst.

Houssara mentioned only one recurring memory, a ghastly one. He was not quite four years old when a Khmer Rouge soldier held a knife to his throat and demanded to know who his father was. Naturally he was frightened and admitted that his father was a Senator. 'How many wives does your father have?' they asked. 'Only my mother,' said Houssara. 'How many houses?' 'Only one.' The child's 'confession' had led to the harsh treatment their father received at the hands of the Khmer Rouge and, indirectly, to his death. Houssara cut himself off from his past completely, so completely that he could not recall it even when he tried. He was, of course, very young but somehow I don't think that was the only reason. When questioned, he would invent wild, cinematic stories of Marines and helicopters with himself wounded and cared for by beautiful blondes. We soon learned not to question him at all. Strangely he is renowned among his friends in Italy for his extraordinary memory. Whenever these aging twenty-three-year-olds want to remember something from their collective past, they call on Houssara. His memory for things since his arrival here is phenomenal.

As for Cambodia, he could understand the anger and the fear of the others but had no thought of revenge or retribution. He was, in fact, the only one of the children who ever talked about going back to Cambodia. The past was too present and too painful for the others to even think of a return. I found it a blessing that Houssara's mind was free to know or not know. What others knew or thought about him never bothered him as it did the older two. He seemed instinctively to understand that there were certain things that he couldn't help people knowing and as for the rest, he didn't care. Young as he was he had made his choice, probably unconscious at first but later a willed, conscious one.

Kilen tried to show a spirit of forgiveness. 'I know Pol Pot doesn't care if I forgive him but I don't care if he doesn't care,' she said. She seemed to feel that forgiveness would put all the horror behind her. Perhaps in the long run it did help but the nightmares continued with the same intensity. Scarcely a night passed without hearing her screams or moans. Is there a point, I wondered, where forgiveness is of no use? She came to me in tears once saying, 'My heart is closed and I'm still bitter.' Kilen had a larger vocabulary than the boys or her mother but many words and expressions came directly from the dictionary. The move to Italy had jolted Kilen: Sary was too depressed to notice; Samreth too busy; Houssara too young for it to be more than a pleasant surprise. But for Kilen it was traumatic. She would wake up in the morning not realizing where she was, a common occurrence to any new arrival, but not knowing if she herself was real. Was this a dream or was the past horror only a nightmare? The change was so rapid, the difference so enormous that she was bewildered and frightened. The absolute newness of it all seemed to strip her of herself. She would walk through the fields near our house and ask aloud, 'Is this freedom? Is this me?' The more her imagination soared the more she craved reality. In those first months she was enormously attached to food and continually overate: as though the fullness of her stomach, even the belly-aches, gave her concrete proof of her existence.

Samreth, on the other hand, longed for revenge, and the bloodier the better. He and Tuyen became friends, after circling around each other for the first few weeks. Their initial distrust was talked away during long night sessions around the dinner table led by our daughter Lisa who explained things in a vaguely dialectical way – she was a Marxist then, although a wildly unorthodox one. For whatever reasons, and I vote for proximity and general goodness, the barriers came down entirely for both families. Tuyen and Samreth had the most bizarre conversations in a mixture of Chinese, Vietnamese and Italian. Each was an expert in the martial arts and they practised Kung Fu among the olive trees. Samreth, suspended in the air, hands splayed and hair flying was amazing and beautiful in his own way, and to see him climb a gigantic live oak as though it were a coconut palm was a treat. I was less charmed by the dexterity with which Tuyen and Samreth handled the Con, two metal bars joined by a chain used in Asian martial arts. It whistled menacingly in the air as they twirled it around with amazing speed. (Houssara had none of these talents and seemed not at all interested.) This martial phase, intense as it was at first, faded and they no longer seemed to need hatred and dreams of vengeance as a shelter and a bond. I was also pleased to note that Samreth and Tuyen no longer talked, with relish it seemed to me, about all the refinements of torture used on the Vietnamese by the Cambodians and vice versa. These two, the gentlest and most sensitive lads, must have felt a certain cruelty was expected of them, at least in talk. Just when I congratulated myself on beginning to understand their culture I heard them launch into a discussion of something they called 'head tea', one of the most complicated and terrifying forms of torture I had ever heard of. I begged them to stop and of course they did, laughing, and clearly thinking me most peculiar.

We put the children in our local schools as soon as possible.

We knew the system well – Simon, after all, had been through it – and we trusted that it would accommodate the Cambodians without any serious problem. The elementary and middle schools of Bagno a Ripoli have such an excellent reputation that couples with young children settle here just for that reason. Houssara was first, entering the third grade with children of his own age. One of the children's mothers said, as she asked if he could come to play at their house, 'He is much in demand.' Even today, at twenty-three, four of his closest friends are boys he first met in the third grade. He is also very much at home with the parents and families of his friends. The elementary school teachers often found him more of a challenge than they were prepared for. He took his shoes and socks off in class, found it impossible to sit still and once lovingly squeezed the breast of a pretty teacher. Instead of becoming a pariah he became a hero, which says something for the imaginations of eight-year-old schoolboys with an Italian Catholic education. His peers actually understood him and his problems better than the elementary school teachers did. One teacher complained to me that she found it difficult to discipline him because his friends would object whenever she tried. Only in Middle School did he find the kind of teacher who really helped him: the Professoressa Scatena. She was a strict disciplinarian, but a just one, and he loved her. Like most children, he loved justice. He never asked for favours, even as a small child: justice was what he craved, without indulgence or apology. John and I liked to watch him, unobserved, when he was hatching an idea. He had a concentration that astounded us. His forehead narrowed with curiosity or widened with joy when he found the answer. Later, as he grew older, conversations on the telephone with his mates were often conducted in mathematical equations as he tried to help them with their homework.

When Kilen and Samreth entered Middle School they

were placed in classes with children younger than themselves. They were both small and delicately built so that there was none of that hulking, overgrown feeling that older children get with their younger peers. That they were both beautiful helped, especially in Italy where physical beauty is valued highly, even demanded. When I registered them with the police I took a year off Kilen's age as I didn't want her to feel too far behind the others. I didn't have the heart, or the courage, to change Samreth's birth date as we found that he was born on the same day as Simon. That seemed a bond not to be tampered with. I didn't realize at the time that I was doing Kilen a disservice. At Khao-I-Dang the officials had already done the same thing in what they considered her best interests. Instead of twelve, she was fourteen when she came to us. This 'lie' preyed on her mind and she finally confessed her true age in tears years later. I blamed myself, yet again, for ignorance and arrogant meddling in the lives of others.

Samreth was instinctively good with numbers and resolved complicated mathematical problems long before he could understand what the teacher was saying. Shortly after he started school he volunteered to go to the blackboard and when he solved a difficult problem the class broke into wild applause. He possessed both charm and intuition and he never lost either. More important still he never overworked the former or depended entirely on the latter. A rich and elderly homosexual friend of ours took a great fancy to Samreth. He was not frightened by homosexuality itself, as he enjoyed the attentions of other gay friends of ours. The courtly exchange of compliments around our dinner table delighted him and he did his share of playful flirting. But this one friend was different. I took all three children to visit his grand home and gardens, and they were enthralled. However, when Samreth saw the magnificent, though gloomy, dining room with the table set for two and realized

he was the only one expected to stay to lunch, he was terrified and refused the invitation. He told me later that he was
scared of not knowing what to talk about, but I think he was
disturbed by the weakness he sensed in the older man.

Samreth had the most extraordinary rapport with
animals. It wasn't just that he was born a Buddhist: it was
Kilen who, in Cambodia, had been the religious one.
Samreth once found a baby owl fallen from its nest. He
adopted him and the bird adored him. They became inseparable and Samreth wore the owl on his shoulder like a fluffy
garment, hand-fed him raw meat, and slept with him until
the bird was old enough to fly away. Only then did he admit,
rather like a new father, that the bird's nocturnal habits had
destroyed his sleep night after night. He managed to bathe
our cat, male and half-wild though he was, in the tub and
then to dry his fur with a hair dryer; the cat followed him
about adoringly even after such a humiliation. He had much
the same effect on teenage girls. We live three kilometers up
a very steep road and more than one pretty girl bicycled or
walked the distance just to see him.

At school Kilen initially had more trouble with her studies
than either of the boys. She worked longer hours than her
brothers and made considerable progress at home with John
and myself. With others she was so terribly shy that whenever a teacher asked her a question, even her name, she giggled uncontrollably and was unable to speak. Her first
scholastic year was a disaster and she had to repeat it. I
learned later that she was thought to be 'wanting' by one
teacher who asked in a faculty meeting that something be
done about her. Fortunately, this teacher found herself vehemently opposed by all the others. This particular teacher
retired after Kilen's first year. The second year she had a
teacher, Professoressa Zanobini, who had an adopted
Filipino nephew. With patience and understanding she was

able to reach Kilen who flowered. Even her dress-sense improved. It was Samreth who understood Italian fashion and style long before Kilen did and some of her earlier 'get-ups' could have caused ridicule from less sensitive peers.

Kilen and Samreth both drew and painted extremely well and their pictures were soon on display at school: that helped, too. Kilen chose French as her foreign language and did well. The students all started out at the same level and her natural ability plus hard work soon took her to the top of the class. Her confidence in her 'public' self grew and at home she terrified Houssara and bossed both her mother and me. In proper Oriental fashion she deferred to Samreth and John. In Cambodia she had been a 'Daddy's girl' and John happily did his best to take Daddy's place. He was delighted with her as a pupil. Once while he was giving her a geography lesson he explained *dolce pendenza* (gentle slope) to her. 'Do you understand?' he asked. She reached over and stroked his expanding tummy and said '*dolce pendenza*'. That became one of our first family jokes: useful and unifying. John only drew the line when she offered to pluck out his beard as she had done for her father. I could not remember when it happened, but soon I could no longer imagine our lives without the Du Caus and the Khuls.

John and I wanted to introduce the children to our own culture as painlessly as possible. The first Easter we concentrated on chocolate eggs and let the rest of the rituals go. Samreth and Kilen decorated lovely hollowed out real eggs the following Easter, some of which I still have. By Christmas we felt that there was enough language and familiarity to do a bit more. The children learned a certain amount about Western culture at school but when Samreth came home one day and wanted to know why everyone laughed when he asked, 'What is a Madonna?' we felt the time had arrived for further instruction. Putting up the creche that first Christmas was a simple beginning. Sary followed the story in her Cambodian translation of the Bible. Moss was gathered, artificial lakes were made, animals were arranged and rearranged, candles were placed in strategic spots. It was a triumph. Then came the tree under the supervision of Simon, home for his school holidays and pleased to share the artistic responsibility. Christmas morning routine is unoriginal and unvarying in our house and I love it. The presents are placed under the tree; John lights a fire in the fireplace; we put carols on the record player; the children pretend to sleep until they are called; Lisa and the Du Caus arrive and then the day begins. Our Christmas is much more about eating, drinking and present-giving than religion but something came across. There had been quite a bit of religious instruction for the residents of the camps as there were missionaries everywhere and everyone had a great deal of time to kill. The missionaries at Khao-I-Dang must have been a sadistic lot though as all Samreth and Houssara could remember from hours of teaching was the Crown of Thorns and the Crucifixion.

John and I have, like most parents, tried to do what we consider the right thing by and for Simon and Lisa. We spent countless hours – John is a theorizer and I am a babbler – discussing how best to help them become independent and responsible. Those hours were as nothing compared to the length of our discussions about the Cambodians. We were frightened, terrified, of not doing the 'right' thing, a fear we hadn't felt before, at least not so strongly.

Love and understanding are seldom, if ever, on the same level, but some recognizable, instinctive reaction to and from one's biological children (I suppose it is DNA or something scientific) makes life less complicated. We did our best to make up for this with the Cambodians with good will on both sides. All three children, in varying degrees, became willing to recognize that there were things they couldn't understand. This, in a strange way, made life not more but less mysterious. Unquestioning acceptance, credulity if you like, can be a terrible weakness in adults but for these children it was an added strength. John and I were aware of their faith in us, and found it unsettling and pleasurable at the same time.

All three had a fierce need for physical contact. I woke up one morning to find Samreth gently stroking my face. Kilen was delighted with the Italian custom of kissing on both cheeks which she practised with the zeal of a convert, shy as she was. And Houssara as a small child was on my lap or John's almost before we sat down. Tradition and culture kept Sary from cuddling her children so they made the most of the strange but comforting Western ways. Having been surrounded and subjected to capricious, unyielding, danger-ous behaviour sharpened the children's sensitivity. Such terrifying circumstances made them both more wary, and more foresighted but fortunately for us, not less trusting, when trust was once given. Trust like affection was offered spontaneously and somehow always at the right moment, like a master chef opening the oven door when the soufflé was at its peak.

Each was capable of fierce anger, even rage. Kilen's was directed at herself for what she felt were unpardonable short-comings. Once she forgot a book at school that she needed in order to prepare the following day's lesson and I came upon her sobbing, pulling her own hair and cursing herself in Cambodian. Samreth's rages, which were terrify-ing but fortunately brief, were against any possible offense or imagined threat to himself or his family. I soon learned to wait until the rage wore itself out. I could no more have stopped it than I could have frozen a waterfall. Houssara grew angry with anyone he suspected of not loving him enough. His flare-ups were often followed by distant and prolonged silences, that dissolved as abruptly as they arrived. As they began to feel safer, all three became more and more in control of their emotions. I remembered all my own irrational and very ordinary childhood fears, but horrifying all the same: the sounds of night, the dark itself, driving past the cemetery, snakes and creeping things of the imagination. If fears independent of experience are real enough to a child, what must the terror born of experience be like? Those stored deep in the memory must surely be the strongest. Houssara still today has a terror of flies anywhere near meat. Not just a normal repulsion but an irrational horror. After my assurances and persuasion Kilen agreed to go for Italian lessons from a sixty-year-old priest in a nearby parish, who had offered to tutor her. She insisted, however, on wearing trousers because of her fear of men. Her sister Poutherein (we had discovered through the Red Cross that she was alive and settled in California), couldn't stop washing her hands she was so worried about germs and for over a year she scrubbed the telephone after each use. It took years of safety to overcome their immediate fears and to allow for a bit of reflection. In some cases they never succeeded.

Our first serious cultural difference came early and unexpectedly. The four Khuls were in the kitchen, John was away and I was in my bedroom at the top of the stairs when I heard a great commotion. I rushed down to find Samreth beating Houssara with the dog's leash and the other two watching passively. Houssara's 'crime', I found out later was that he hadn't been studying enough. I stopped Samreth and did my best to explain that we did things differently. I learned that in Cambodia older children had a 'right', even a duty to beat the younger ones. Samreth never hit his brother again although he was sometimes sorely tempted. Houssara told me years later that he was never afraid of Samreth, but that Kilen terrified him when he was small. I tried to teach them the idea of right and wrong as opposed to good and evil, but for children who had lived under the sign of evil it was not a simple concept. Good, they understood as Buddhists, and God knows they had experience enough of evil. But it was not easy for them to grasp the distinction between these absolutes and an everyday sense of good and bad behaviour, or the fact that a simple, human transgression need not be exorcized or beaten out of the culprit like an act of evil. I don't know if I ever got this concept across completely. I do think I convinced them that the aberration of the Khmer Rouge was an evil of the past and no longer the fourth dimension in their lives. If I could make no promises about life or the future, at least I could promise they were safe from that particular horror.

Kilen was the most articulate, and told me stories of her life in Cambodia that usually ended with us both in tears. She also had the worst, or at least the most discernible, nightmares: I often heard her screams during the night. Houssara never cried. He was seldom distressed but if he was he would curl up on the floor like a wounded animal and sleep, sometimes for hours and hours. Sary hadn't cried, she said, since her little girl of nine died. She had black depressions and told me she longed to cry but couldn't. The strangest thing finally unblocked her. There was a programme on Italian television that the children loved, a rather dreadful adventure series based on a book by Salgari (a turn-of-the-century hack) called 'Sandokan'. It was shot in Malaysia, and like most Italian films, was lovely to look at. The children adored the indomitable hero played by an incredibly handsome Indian actor and persuaded Sary to watch it with them. The setting was so reminiscent of Cambodia – the clothes, the rivers, the trees, and the different plants, all of which she kept pointing out to them with sighs of pleasure – that she began to cry. We all cheered and cheered.

I found myself telling moralising stories to engage the children's imagination. They recognized the underlying truths even without completely understanding the stories. Once after such a tale I said to Kilen 'You see, how things change, you won't always be in this position.' She said, 'I won't be anywhere always.' What the past had done to their imaginations I never really found out. To me it was remarkable that none of them brought away anything of those terrible times except the suffering. What I mean is that since children, all children, learn by imitation, and since language itself, behaviour and habits are all acquired that way, they might easily have picked up something of the viciousness or falseness that surrounded them. Evil is so much easier to imitate than good: war can be imitated easily, peace less so. But despite everything they had seen or known they somehow still hoped, even expected, that good would be done to them. They had an uncritical and touching faith in 'America', the America of their dreams, the America of their father's promises. Their father had spent some time in California as a student and year by year the family myth grew until America became another name for the Great Good Place. When our politically minded daughter, Lisa, finally got Samreth and Kilen to 'boo' an appearance of Kissinger on the television she felt she had really accomplished something. It was not until they actually went to America that their attitudes changed and became more realistic.

Sary had grown up in a static society in which most people lived and died where they were born and where her sense of her own value was determined by birth. She was less dis-

66

turbed by what the children perceived as social injustice. It was easier for her to accept things as they were, not for any rational or moral reason, but just because they were. I know little about Buddhism but I suspect its teachings had something to do with her resignation and acceptance. Cambodian beliefs seemed to me unique: a mixture of Buddhism, old Hindu rites and folklore. Added to this was the combination of magic and black arts practised by the Chams, the largest indigenous minority in the country. Many Cambodians from Phnom Penh visited the Cham community on the peninsula where the Mekong River meets the inland sea, Tonle Sap. They went to seek predictions for the future, to obtain love-potions or help in eliminating rivals. Even the educated and the most sophisticated Cambodians had a respect for, if not a complete belief in, magic. Even among the Buddhist monks there were fortune-tellers and astrologers. Each regiment of soldiers had its own *Lok Kru* or magician whose spells and potions were supposed to make them invulnerable in battle. Lon Nol's more bizarre actions must have resulted from a magician's prompting: he was a firm believer and there is certainly no rational explanation for some of his behaviour. Sary herself was adept at telling the future (the children consulted her before exams) and interpreting dreams. Sary said that in Buddhist reincarnation the highest stage one could reach, before sainthood, was to become 'an Englishman'.

Each in his own way had been saddened, stunned or strengthened by survival. Sary had lost the most. When she came to Italy she was forty-three and within the last five years most of her family had been destroyed. She repeated this litany of her terrible losses with the constancy and devotion of a woman telling the beads in her Rosary. Sary had been born, privileged, into a world without change and had assumed that the world would continue to hold still so that her children could grow up in it, too. The abrupt, convulsive, upheaval in Cambodia, unforeseen by many people, was yet another incomprehensible burden for her to bear.

Towards the end of April the weather improved and with it Sary's spirits. The children's enthusiasm and obvious happiness was infectious and Sary began to smile more and more often. Not those forced smiles that make the lips look thin and the eyes disappear, but real, relaxed, joyful smiles. She was a beautiful woman and Tuyen, who had become the unofficial head of all Asian refugees in our part of Tuscany, was asked by a fellow Cambodian to arrange an introduction. After the first meeting he made her an offer of marriage. The refugee was a widower and she was not surprised, just not at all interested. She was not ready to re-marry she told me. Furthermore, from his use of language she knew him to be a former member of the Khmer Rouge. The offer was politely but decisively refused.

At first I drove everyone to school but soon the children were ready for the adventure of the school bus. The bright yellow *Scuolabus*, driven by alternating bearded youths, both named Roberto, was a constant in our valley: clocks were set when the high-pitched horn announced its arrival. Since we live far out in the country the children were collected early and had one of the longest bus rides. They made friends easily and were soon familiar with the expressions, phrases, including some stunning swear words, that children everywhere pick up from their peers. They also learned local customs, fads and taste. Some fads they refused: none of them liked Italian pop music or mini-skirts. Samreth disliked the noise in discotheques although he was a Michael Jackson fan early on. His friends accepted these heresies and in many cases followed Samreth's lead.

Preparing for the eight o'clock school bus was no longer the panic it was at first. Routine was a great help in allaying anxiety. I watched with fascination as each child patched together structures that would help meet all these new challenges. Consciously or not, each built a separate identity complete with his own idiosyncrasies. Family jokes are, I realized, very helpful in such situations. The beginning of the day was important. I had tried, and failed, to teach them about the Western idea of breakfast. As a child I had hated breakfast and even now I take only caffe latte, so perhaps I wasn't the best teacher but I don't think the lesson would have worked even with a British cooked breakfast enthusiast. They preferred to eat meat or fish with rice or noodles together with the ubiquitous *Nuc Mam* fish sauce. I stayed out of the kitchen as they ate their morning meal and opened all the windows when they left. Each child had distinct food preferences: Kilen ate everything except strawberries which gave her hives; Samreth loved raw vegetables and steak; Houssara would eat any variety of fish at any time of day. There was never any danger of addiction to cokes or junk food, thank God, and Samreth and Kilen were excellent cooks.

Kilen always sat at the very back of the bus, at first out of shyness and later because it had become her place. The second year she had a group of girls who vied for the seat next to her. We bought Samreth a motorbike for his birthday so he felt independent and much more mature. This was never resented by the other two, after all he was 'first born'. Italian law allows a 50cc motorbike at fourteen, so Houssara knew all he had to do was wait. Not so Kilen who, after a disastrous experiment with a bicycle, had decided against anything with two wheels. Samreth was a natural trendsetter although he could not be called a leader: he was too suspicious of any organization, even his own. His successes with girls continued until he found real love with a fellow student at art school. Then neither he nor she had eyes or time for anyone else. Their romance was well known at school and applauded and encouraged by their fellow students. Also, to my surprise, by the girl's mother.

All three children were generous with their affections and straightforward with their emotions (sometimes too much so). Each child had a willingness to part with anything he was fond of that I found unusual. They grew naturally, never taking more than they needed – like young trees that grow taller and thinner for their share of sunlight.

PART III

From five years of punishment for an offence
  It took America five years to commit
These victim-children have been released on parole.
  They will remember all of it.

FIRST CAME THE musicians – eight because the Sous were an important family – then Sary's brothers and her father, then her mother walking alone followed by Sary herself with her four attendants supporting an embroidered canopy over her head, all walking slowly to her new home, the home of her husband. An old Cambodian custom decreed that the bride be secluded for fifteen days before her marriage. The first week she was completely covered with a paste whose basic ingredient was turmeric, to make her skin paler and more beautiful.

Sary's wedding took place when she was eighteen. Her mother, who had married at fifteen, had supervised the match, although the choice was Sary's. Her family was prominent – her father ran the Cambodian postal system, and they were well-off. As Sary was lovely it was not surprising that there were several suitors. She told me, proudly, that she had chosen Sarin Khul (or Khul Sarin as she called him in the Cambodian fashion) for his intelligence and his gentleness. She had never been alone with him before they were married and had only seen him a few times.

The marriage was a success not only for the six children it produced. They had a real companionship, unusual in an Oriental marriage. Sarin was a teacher, journalist and senator. Sary spent a great deal of time with her husband and was interested and well informed about politics, meeting many of the local leaders and foreign diplomats. Sarin taught her how to smoke cigarettes so that she would feel more at ease, he said, with foreign wives. Her political views may have been simplistic – she found it hard to believe that their old friend, Khieu Sampan, who gave his money to the poor and lived a simple austere life, could sanction Khmer Rouge brutality. Sarin had no such illusions: 'You must realize,' he said, 'that Khieu has begun to dress like a cowboy.' Everything was symbolic in Cambodia, then as in the past, and Khieu Sampan's new dress code revealed the shift in his politics.

By all accounts Sarin was a remarkable man: intelligent, honourable and, under the circumstances, patriotic to the point of folly. Many times he could have escaped Cambodia but he felt it his duty to stay in his country and fight the regime in power – first Sihanouk and then the Khmer Rouge. Sarin sought unselfish and impartial justice: he was vehemently and outspokenly opposed to the prevalent corruption. As a journalist he spared no one in his condemnation and as a senator, he spoke out whenever possible. Appalled when he learned that food the Red Cross intended for refugees from the countryside was stolen and sold on the black market, he mobilized family and friends. Even the children were enrolled. When a group of lorries carrying rice, sugar, salt and dried fish arrived, Sarin rode 'shotgun' on the lead lorry and placed friends or relatives on the others to ensure their safe arrival at the destined government enclaves. The children remember one particular day when they were allowed to help in the distribution of food. Sarin and the other men rode up front in the cabs with the drivers while the women and children were bundled in the back with the supplies. No one wanted to ride in the lorry carrying the dried fish but all the others were full. The caravan was noisy and joyous. They went far from Phnom Penh near to an old temple. Journalists and colleagues Sarin had asked to be present gave the day an air of importance as well as festivity.

The children were so proud of the way their father took charge. Young as they were they could not help noticing the respect and admiration of the refugees – this was obviously not his first trip. The women measured out the food and the men distributed it from the back of the lorries. Poutherein, the eldest daughter, even today remembers her feelings of pride mixed with jealousy. Strangers seemed to be witnessing her father's love in a stronger form than she had ever experienced.

She and Samreth, who were less than a year apart in age, had planned on selling the empty food sacks and asked their father's permission. Sarin, the untainted, refused them saying that the sacks must go back to the Red Cross. The children argued that surely an organization as huge and important as the Red Cross had no need for empty sacks while they could sell them for quite a bit of money. Busy as he was, Sarin stopped everything and gave them a lecture on the beginning of corruption. Their anger and disappointment at the time was acute. Now the story is told with pride, an important part of the family legend. Sarin, with his fearless integrity, was the kind of man who might well begin a reform movement or even a revolution and yet be one of its first victims. The impartial, the humane and the unselfish cannot for long be leaders of a violent movement.

Much contemporary Cambodian history is bound up in the person of Norodom Sihanouk, who was crowned king in 1941 and remained in power in one form or another until 1970. In 1955, in an astute political move, he abdicated the throne in favour of his father. That way he could stand for the elections due to take place by the terms of the Geneva Peace Accord. No longer a monarch he now referred to himself as a politician of the people and he scored an overwhelming victory at that year's polls. He then ruled as Prince through his father. He also ruled as Prime Minister and

Chief of State. Not content with that he was also a film director, magazine editor, saxophone-playing jazz-band leader and ran the country's lucrative gambling concession. After his electoral victory Sihanouk became more and more autocratic but he never succeeded in uniting his country. In his memoirs, *My War with the CIA*, he says that he did not think it necessary for Cambodia to imitate Western-style democracy with its multi-party system. He reserved his strongest criticism for the educated middle class, describing them as 'Neither Prince nor People'. Understandably the intellectuals drifted away from Phnom Penh, the more conservative members to join Son Ngoc Than's Khmer Serei, those of the left to join the Communist underground.

Sihanouk encouraged American aid to his country in the late fifties and early sixties. However, when he began to suspect that many of his ministers and generals were becoming dependent on American help and, even worse, absorbing American ideas, he began to reconsider his position. He was undoubtedly angered at the South Vietnamese raids into Cambodian territory that began in 1958 and enraged when he learned that weapons supplied by American aid could not be used to oppose the invaders. American aid, he was told, was for the purpose of repelling Communist aggression only. Meanwhile border disputes continued with the United States supporting its clients, Saigon and Bangkok. A South Vietnamese incursion into Stung Treng Province (in the Northeast near both Laos and Vietnam) in 1958 brought a vigorous protest from Cambodia to the International Control Commission but nothing was done and border violations continued. It was not until 1965 that the ICC published a report accusing South Vietnam of hundreds of violations of Cambodian territory in 1964 and 1965. The Commission concluded that not a single raid was provoked by Cambodia.

As well as his desire to maintain Cambodian neutrality, Sihanouk had a respect and admiration for the Vietnamese who were fighting 'American aggression'. He was the only head of state to attend Ho Chi Minh's funeral in Hanoi in 1969. Sihanouk had reason to suspect that American policy was to encourage raids by both Thais and South Vietnamese, thus putting pressure on him to request American intervention in Cambodia. He reacted, totally in character, in quite the opposite way: he began to forge ties with Peking. The assassination of President Diem of South Vietnam in 1963 must have come as a shock to Sihanouk. Shortly afterwards he began an uncharacteristic program of nationalisation and economic reform, swinging sharply to the left. He became convinced that Hanoi was winning the war in Vietnam and moved in accordance. Then in 1963 he took a dramatic and daring step by rejecting the American Aid program that had been in effect since 1955 and demanding that all aid missions be closed and all Embassy personnel sent home. He gave as his official reason the United States' support of his old enemy Son Ngoc Than. His rejection of American aid was not universally approved in Phnom Penh. Some American officials sensed this and made contact with the then Minister of Defense and Chief of Police, Lon Nol. When the head of the American military mission paid his farewell visit to the ministry, he was assured by Lon Nol of his friendship, and the support of the troops under his direct command. This information was relayed to Washington. The White House did not ignore Lon Nol's offer: it was accepted, and eventually acted upon with dire results.

The definitive break between Cambodia, in the person of Sihanouk, and the United States did not come until May of 1965, following closely upon the landing of the American Marines in South Vietnam. Even before this Sihanouk had allowed the North Vietnamese forces to use the bordering zones between Cambodia and South Vietnam as military bases. This, in turn, led to more extensive border raids carried out by South Vietnamese and Americans into Cambodian territory. Shortly after the inauguration of Richard Nixon as president secret bombing missions were begun by the United States. The targets were the North Vietnamese bases within Cambodian territory but it was inevitable that Cambodian civilians, mostly peasants, were also killed. Cambodian peasants, unlike their Vietnamese neighbours, were not accustomed to bombing. To isolated, semi-literate, superstitious people these raids must have seemed like works of black magic; nothing human could possibly effect such destruction.

Imperious as only an hereditary Southeast Asian king could be, Sihanouk was a brilliant, if unscrupulous, politician. He shrewdly played Chinese, American and Soviet interests against each other. In public statements he maintained that he never wanted Cambodia to become a Communist country and sent his troops against the Khmer Rouge even as he was moving closer and closer to Hanoi. He had in the past, when expedient, worked with French colonial rulers and with Japanese conquerors. He was surrounded by sycophants whom he lavishly rewarded when he was pleased. He accepted little advice, absolutely no criticism and often indulged in temper tantrums. His face was round, boyish and unlined; his voice squeaky and excited; his charm, like his volatility, undeniable (he was known to the popular American press as 'Snooky'). To his credit he tried to maintain Cambodia's neutrality and to oppose, by any means, the extension of war in Southeast Asia. American concern with Sihanouk's neutrality grew as American involvement in Vietnam increased. His largely successful policy of 'extreme neutrality' was never accepted in powerful circles within Cambodia and Washington. Opposition to this policy eventually brought about his downfall.

Sarin Khul was opposed to the corruption of Sihanouk's court. He was a follower of Son Ngoc Than and very pro-American. Relatively little has been written about Son Ngoc Than, but he was an important figure in Cambodia during the struggle against French colonialism in the thirties and forties. He was the first modern intellectual proponent of Khmer nationalism, began the first Khmer language newspaper and was a leader in the effort to modernize Cambodia and turn it into a democracy. Than was called 'the father of the Cambodian independence movement' by many. Sihanouk however always referred to him as a 'traitor'. It is true that he collaborated with the Japanese during World War II (he was Prime Minister under a Japanese-sponsored government in 1945) and is reported to have collaborated with the CIA from 1958 to 1970. The former in the hopes of freeing Cambodia from French domination, the latter in ridding the country of the Monarchy's absolute rule. Than's movement attracted many of the educated middle-class who were inspired by his opposition to corruption, colonialism and absolute monarchy.

Sihanouk considered Son Ngoc Than a Communist and sneered at his followers as 'intellectuals'. Son Ngoc Than's movement was undercut when Cambodia obtained its independence from France in 1953. The fledgling Cambodian Communist Party was also decimated. At the Geneva Peace Conference in 1954 Cambodia's neutrality was recognized and both Hanoi and Peking agreed that the minuscule force of Cambodian Communists (later to be called the Khmer Rouge) be disbanded and its members sent to Hanoi. 'Proletarian solidarity' was not a serious concern to the negotiators of the treaty. A few Cambodian Communists remained in the jungle where they had been operating but several thousand were sent to Hanoi. Those who remained in the jungle, and those who came to join them later, considered this a betrayal, a betrayal that was neither forgotten nor forgiven. Even the official date of the founding of the Party was changed. Formerly the date had been 1951 when the Lao Dong (Workers') Party was formed in Vietnam, now it was decreed that 1960 was the actual date of the birth of the Khmer Rouge. The Party's leaders and their followers sought to distance themselves from any Vietnamese influence. In 1963 a small group, led by Saloth Sar, as Pol Pot was still called then, went underground in the jungle and there they lived until their final victory. They left behind them a reputation for honesty and anti-corruption. It was they who formed the leadership of the Khmer Rouge, bound together by blood and marital ties and the French education that most of them had received. In 1967 Sihanouk's forces crushed a left-wing revolt in the province of Battambang. Some of the surviving leaders fled to the bush to join those already there, among them Khieu Sampan, Hu Nim and Hou Youn, all of whom had held important positions in Sihanouk's government. Power remained in the hands of Pol Pot and the men and women of 1963 and with the exception of Khieu Sampan, the others had little influence or were eliminated.

Sihanouk, denouncing the super-powers America and the Soviet Union as 'depraved', collaborated with the North Vietnamese. In 1963 he allowed them to establish base camps along Cambodia's border with South Vietnam and to ship supplies through the port of Sihanoukville. It was Sihanouk's policy to play off the rival factions within the country in the same way that he encouraged foreign influences to compete for his favour. However, his sagacity and maneuvering were not enough to protect his country. Opposing forces were too strong and he failed. His power was based upon an almost mystical communion with the Cambodian peasants to whom he was a semi-divinity, and whose support and affection he never lost. Typically, he used this attachment to his own advantage. When making an unpopular decision he placed the blame on the indignation of the peasants whose wishes, he claimed, were sacred. Because Cambodia remained essentially a feudal kingdom he was, however, unable to subdue the warlords, local chiefs and rich landowners who held power in various parts of the land.

In spite of his capricious and erratic behaviour Sihanouk was constant on one important issue: opposition to America's attempt to bring Cambodia further into the war in Southeast Asia. In spite of outside pressure he refused (in 1956) to join the American-sponsored Southeast Asia Treaty Organization (SEATO). This brought him into conflict with Lon Nol and Prince Sirik Matak, as representatives of the officer corps and the political and business elite. The White House backed Lon Nol, and the coup which deposed Sihanouk took place in 1970 while Sihanouk himself was out of the country. He learned of the coup as he was being taken to the airport in Moscow for a flight to Peking. On arrival in China he was met by Chou En-lai and accorded the honours of a head of state. Within a few days Sihanouk announced that he had formed a National Front of Kampuchea together with the Khmer Rouge to fight Lon Nol. He received pledges of support from the Viet Cong, the North Vietnamese, the Pathet Lao and eventually, the Chinese. Sihanouk did not return to his country for three years.

In April that year the border raids gave way to a full-scale invasion by South Vietnamese and American forces – an invasion not sanctioned by the United States Congress, unknown to most Americans and disastrous for all con-cerned. The struggle between President Nixon and Congress increased. The American Congress had a proviso in every military appropriation bill that prohibited bombing Cambodia except to protect Americans in Vietnam. By 1973 there were no longer any Americans left there but the bombing did not stop. The White House continued to abuse its power and gave as justification the need to eliminate North Vietnamese troops who were poised to conquer South Vietnam. Not until late in 1973 was Congress able to withhold funds and stop the bombing of Cambodia.

The coup that brought Lon Nol to power vastly increased corruption. Graft was nothing new in Cambodia but with the advent of American military aid it became monumental. Some Embassy officials in Phnom Penh urged America to pressure Lon Nol to end, or at least, curb the corruption but the White House paid no attention. Lon Nol became more and more dictatorial, taking counsel only from the White House or his 'spiritual advisers'. At one point he arrested his closest and most important collaborator, Prince Sirik Matak, who had dared criticize the government. In an interview to the *New York Times* Sirik Matak warned America that the Lon Nol regime could not last and that if nothing was done Cambodia would fall to the Communists. He, too, was ignored. One American Embassy official said Lon Nol seemed to have been chosen only for his incompetence. All through 1974, the American Ambassador, John Gunther Dean, urged Kissinger to negotiate a 'controlled solution'. This would mean removing Lon Nol from power, requesting the return of Sihanouk, and arranging a truce with the Khmer Rouge. The White House, once again, refused to listen until it was too late. Sihanouk's insistence on Cambodian neutrality was one of the excuses given for his overthrow and replacement by Lon Nol. That and what was known as 'The Nixon Doctrine in its purest form.' Senator George McGovern, an outspoken critic of the war in Indo-China, put it bluntly when he was quoted by U.P.I. in 1971 – the

Nixon Doctrine meant 'We pay them for killing each other.'

Before the Khmer Rouge victory Cambodia became a dangerous place for Sarin. He made enemies among important members of Sihanouk's government. Sarin's good friend, the Japanese Ambassador, offered to take the two older girls (Kilen and Poutherein) to Tokyo for safety but he refused to separate the family. It was a decision he came to regret and later when the misery was greater, he admitted that separation would have been a better choice. I thought about Anne Frank and how the desire for unity destroyed that family, too. Sarin determined to teach his family how to survive in the country. He had been born in Kompong Thom in the centre of Cambodia, north of the great inland sea, Tonle Sap. Kompong Thom was also the birthplace of Pol Pot and Deuch, the head of the notorious death camp, Tuol Sleng. Sarin understood the 'other' Cambodia, the land that was not part of the fertile, rice-growing, Buddhist-loving section along the Mekong River and Tonle Sap. One of the most primitive 'other' regions, the land of the Kuy, a wild and forested area, lay merely a few kilometers north of Kompong Thom. He insisted on lessons in survival: what edible foods could be found in the woods; the use of natural herbal remedies, the boiling of certain flowers as a cure for sunstroke, grasses that could be used as poultices to draw out infection, the bark of a tree that when boiled produced a liquid that could reduce swelling. He taught Samreth how to fish and Samreth's fondest and deepest memories of his father are the days they spent together on the river. This was the first theme Samreth wrote about in Italian and he was furious when the teacher considered it not a serious subject for an essay. Kilen loved quoting her father, her first efforts in Italian were towards interpreting his words. She kept repeating one of his favorite phrases, 'If you die today, you don't have to die tomorrow.' This seemed to her a great comfort.

Samreth had a more complex memory of his father. The mixture of pride and anger with which Samreth spoke of him was in marked contrast with Kilen's worship or Houssara's ignorance (he scarcely knew his father). Sary's first pregnancy had ended in miscarriage and Samreth (her second) was born at seven months, shortly after the death of Sarin's father. The night of Sarin's father's death Sary had dreamed of seven stars and seven bolts of golden cloth. According to Buddhist belief Samreth was the reincarnation of his paternal grandfather and there was no question in Sary's mind that this was the case.

Houssara was born in July of 1972 when the American bombardment of Cambodia had been in operation for over two years. Fortunately for Sary it was an uncomplicated birth. The North Vietnamese bases had been damaged but not destroyed and they were moved farther and farther into the interior of Cambodia. As a result the range of the bombing was notably increased, resulting in more and more civilian casualties. Refugees from the countryside were streaming into the bloated, decaying city of Phnom Penh. They were trying to escape death from the blanket bombings which were destroying large sections of rural Cambodia. The wounded staggered into the city, often dragging the broken bodies of their comrades, in the vain hope of help. The hospitals were no better than medieval pesthouses with three or four patients to a bed or lying, with their wounds untreated, on the filthy floor. Treatment, when available, was rudimentary and often brutal: there was no anaesthetic left in any hospital, and the few available medicines were to be found only on the black market at highly inflated prices, where gold was the only accepted exchange.

Conditions in the Khul household were less horrifying but life must have been incredibly difficult for them all, especially Sary. Sarin was busy helping the refugees and she was left in charge of the household consisting of her parents, her two younger sisters and six children, aged from a recently born infant to a boy of eleven. Sarin would drive every day to the edge of town where broken down buses brought a pitiful tide of refugees from the countryside. There he would collect families laden with what possessions they were able to salvage and drive them to the city, several miles away. If they were fortunate and had relatives he would see them settled. In most cases the new arrivals had no place to go and Sarin took them to the overcrowded government enclaves and found them a place there. On an average day he would settle seven or eight families that way. It was, he said, only a gesture, a sign that these wretched people were not totally forgotten: to the refugees it must certainly have seemed much more. Sarin's integrity (or foolhardiness) was severely tested by circumstances. One refugee family, hearing of his efforts, came to the house in tears. They had, they told him, lost everything in the bombing and were now living in a government enclave. There they had planted vegetables and built a shack to make a temporary home for their seven children. They had just learned that they were to be turned out as the land was being leased to the Americans: once again they had nowhere to go. The profit, and it would surely be enormous, from the lease was going directly to the Commander in Chief of the Cambodian army. Since the country was under martial law there seemed no recourse. Sarin's sense of justice and duty obliged him to act no matter what dangers were involved. He took his camera and with Sary driving the car, circled about the land carefully photographing the plight of the refugees with a special emphasis on the food plots. Then, bolder and more imprudent than ever, he went to the American Embassy. There he found a sympathetic and evidently important member of staff. 'You are here to help Cambodia, are you not?' asked Sarin. The Embassy official assured him that was certainly his personal intention as well as government policy. Sarin told him the story of the refugees and showed the photographs he had taken. The official was surprised – by his ignorance or his innocence – he had believed the land to be often flooded and unused swamp land. The result was that the deal was called off and the refugees were no longer forced to move. Sarin had requested that his name not be mentioned, but that was evidently asking too much. The story was all over Phnom Penh within a few days and Sarin had made another powerful enemy.

The years that followed 1972 were even more destructive. The massive American–South Vietnamese bombardment intended to destroy the Khmer Rouge only strengthened their resolve and made them more unyielding, more extreme. Peasant boys and girls, slimy and cold and huddled in hastily dug, muddy trenches were pounded day and night by the most powerful and sophisticated weapons. Fatal casualties in some units were as high as fifty per cent. Almost miraculously they edged forward: an under-equipped, brutalized force many of whom were still in their teens. They somehow pushed on to the capital commanded, urged and driven by a handful of jungle-hardened leaders. They laid siege to Phnom Penh itself, first blocking the Mekong so that no supplies could get through. Food became scarce, medical supplies exhausted, but the city was saved from famine by an American airlift of food. The city avoided capitulation in 1973 and 1974 only thanks to the arrival of the rainy season, and possibly the Khmer Rouge's lack of ammunition.

The final assault of the Khmer Rouge began on January 1, 1975, the onset of the dry season. The circle around the city tightened and by March they were within one mile of the Pochentong airport. The airlift of food and ammunition was suspended. On 12 April John Gunther Dean, the American Ambassador, announced the evacuation of all American officials. He offered places on the waiting helicopters to members of the Cambodian government or politicians who wished to join him. Unlike Vietnam the retreat was orderly, 82 Americans, 159 Cambodians and 35 other nationals left without incident. Astonishingly few Cambodians accepted his offer. Matak (Sihanouk's cousin and one-time ally of Lon Nol) decided to stay behind although his name was high on the Khmer Rouge's death list. He made his way, together with about eight hundred foreigners and over six hundred Cambodians, to the French embassy which was the only Embassy still open. The conquerors refused to recognize extra-territorial status or diplomatic privilege and demanded that all Cambodians within the Embassy be surrendered immediately. Failure to do so would ensure that all foreigners would be subject to summary 'justice'. The French officials had no choice. Khmer Rouge vengeance when it came was swift and terrible.

Despite the blow of American abandonment, the government soldiers kept on fighting. They fought without their officers, without ammunition, without food and without hope. The government finally surrendered on 15 April and 17 April saw the triumphal entry of the Khmer Rouge into Phnom Penh. Most people thought the war was over. That first day there was dancing and celebration.

Early on the morning of 15 April during the Cambodian New Year the Khul family heard shouting in the streets. Samreth went out on his bicycle and came home to report a white flag flying over the barracks nearby. 'Turn on the radio,' said Sary. There they heard that the government of Lon Nol (who was himself safely out of the country) was to surrender and people were told to hang out white flags. Then there was a call for all military and civilian physicians and surgeons as well as all medical students to report at once to the medical reception centre at Borei Keila (Olympic) Stadium. The family had two close friends who were doctors. They learned later that one reported, one did not. Neither survived. This announcement was followed by the regular Buddhist prayers – that day they lasted longer than usual – and then by martial music. Afterwards the radio went dead. Soon the house was filled with aunts, uncles, cousins and close friends. The children were surprised when they were sent away so that there could be a meeting of the adults and some of the excitement began to wear off. Sary's uncle, Khy Tang Lim, an important minister, was troubled; no one knew what to expect.

When the Khmer Rouge marched into Phnom Penh on the morning of April 17, 1975, people lined the streets to welcome them. They were so young, these soldiers, so ragged, so gaunt, not at all Samreth's idea of conquerors. The cheers were genuine, people believed the war was over at last. Sary and her family were no exception. Only Sarin was apprehensive when he heard of the approaching army. He left home at four in the morning to help some friends from parliament (whose names were on the Khmer Rouge death list) make their way to a safe hiding place. Because of his liberal record and published opposition to Sihanouk and Lon Nol, he believed that neither he nor his family would be in any immediate danger. Agents of Sihanouk had tried to kill him after he had written a scathing attack in the *Courier Phnompenois* against government corruption. He accused, with proof, some of Lon Nol's officers of stealing the pay of the soldiers under their command. The article had caused a sensation and surely made its way to the Khmer Rouge hideaway in the jungle. His instructions to Sary, however, showed a lingering doubt. He told her that at the first signs of trouble she was to take her parents and the children to

Kompong Thom and he would rejoin them there. 'What signs, what trouble?' she wanted to know.

'If they have been too long in the bush, you'll know,' he said. He took off his eyeglasses, buried his books and papers, put on short trousers and left before dawn promising to be back in a few hours.

The family had no chance to act on Sarin's instructions. Almost at once the young, unsmiling victors put into practice their own fearful plan. First they ordered the evacuation of the hospitals. Shivering with fever, bloated by disease, maimed by bombardments, patients were forced out of hospitals all over the city. Cripples led the blind, parents carried their children in plastic bags, those who had strength pushed the beds of the dying. Then attention was turned to the Hotel Phnom where the Red Cross had tried to establish a neutral zone. It too was emptied of workers and wounded alike. The next day Khmer Rouge soldiers went from house to house to evacuate the residents and to send them, if possible, back to the towns of their birth. Khmer Rouge troops converged on the city from different sections of the country and there seemed to be no clear chain of command. The soldiers who controlled the centre section of the city where the Khul family lived came from the Southwest part of the country. These troops were the most disciplined but also the most radical and fierce. The Khul family was told that the move was necessary to save their lives since the Americans were preparing a mammoth bombardment. The Khmer Rouge soldiers posed as saviours in this part of the city. They also said that the move was for only three days or at most a week until all dangers had passed.

Sary, her parents, children and sisters were sent to the village where Sary's mother had been born. Sary's mother at first refused to leave but was finally persuaded to do so. Her eventual death from malnutrition and overwork weighed heavily on Sary's conscience. There was, however, no alternative but to insist that she accompany them. The old and the sick who were left behind perished without exception, and perished alone. Samreth brought out his bicycle and loaded it with food. He was teased by the others for always thinking of his stomach but when they found there was no food along the road they were all grateful to him. Sary, her two younger sisters and the older children loaded her brother's car with valuables, clothes and three fifty-pound sacks of rice – Sarin had taken the family car the morning before. Then they all pushed the car. The car was full of petrol – Sarin had prepared for the worst – but it was impossible to drive. Over a million (some estimates claim that there were as many as two-and-a-half million people involved), inhabitants of Phnom Penh swarmed out of their homes, their hospitals, huts and enclaves at the same time. The Khmer Rouge allowed only one exit from the city. The streets were clogged with people, many of whom had brought their animals with them, all struggling hopelessly to move forward – a stampede in slow motion. It was easy to get lost, some children were tied to their parents. People who fell or staggered were left where they fell and even trampled on. When the evacuees asked where they were to find food and medicine they heard the *Angka* would provide.

The *Angka* (Organization) or *Angka Loeu* (Supreme Organization) had taken over their lives. Orders from the *Angka* conveyed through the fierce young soldiers must be obeyed immediately and without complaint. The old Cambodia was finished. Year zero of Democratic Kampuchea had begun. Although it was only a short distance conditions on the road were so chaotic it took them weeks to arrive. They crept along always guarded and commanded by boys and girls dressed in black with red scarves, carrying Kalashnikovs. Shots were fired from time to time to keep the crowd moving or just to frighten them. They were driven like cattle. Samreth who, like most boys of his age, was fond of Westerns thought that the guards modeled themselves on cowboys. People and animals dragged along, slept, ate and relieved themselves on the road. The elderly, the sick and the very young died there, too, and the bodies were left by the roadside for the Khmer Rouge to collect. The city was divided and some evacuations were harsher than others; often people had only ten minutes to collect their possessions and move out. The real purpose (there were no American bombs) was twofold; to empty the hated city of those who had prospered while they, the new rulers, lived like animals in the jungle; and to make it easier to check on people's backgrounds in the towns where they, or their parents, were born. Another factor was the small number of Khmer Rouge forces. The estimated size in the entire country was sixty to seventy thousand men and women, many untrained and still in their teens. A force that small would have great difficulty controlling a city of well over one million inhabitants, which together with the government enclaves brought the total population to around three million. The family was told that they were to be sent to the village where Sarin's great-grandmother was born. The Khmer Rouge program was to eliminate or make agricultural labourers of all the 'soft city folk', as they were called. Only that way could the perfect new society begin in earnest.

When the evacuees arrived in their designated part of the country they were called 'New People' to distinguish them from the peasants or 'Old People' who had always lived in the zone. During the evacuation Samreth was a great help: he was small and agile, swift and unafraid. Once, when the grandmother complained of thirst he waited until their guards weren't looking, jumped over a fence and shinned up a coconut palm. From that vantage point he saw a terrible sight not visible from the road. There were two old men, one lying, one barely sitting by another tree: they had obviously been abandoned. The stronger of the two lifted a hand to signal to Samreth, the second was too far gone even to do that. The family couldn't understand why Samreth was crying as he brought them the precious coconuts.

After two days on the road Sary realized that they were not going to be given any food at all. They were unable to cook their rice as there was neither space nor firewood. They had only gone a short distance so she decided to make her way back to the house and collect some foodstuffs. She saw smoke coming from fires in the city, she heard cries and whimpers from the innocent victims and thought she detected menacing shouts from the conquerors. On her way back to her family Sary learned far worse. As she was struggling along the road she heard an infant's cry coming from an abandoned house. Pushing and shoving her way through the crowd she finally reached the house, which had been a day care centre. The adults in the house had been forcibly evacuated and the babies under their care deserted. No one was allowed to move independently in the city so the mothers of these infants could not come to collect them. It was mercilessly hot, the infants had probably not been fed since the evacuation two days before and those left with any strength were wailing. The babies were naked and piled together in the centre of a large room. Sary said that they looked like so many fish squirming in the heat. She picked up one under each arm hoping to save at least these two. When she got to the road a boy in black threatened her with his AK-47 and made her take them back. She never learned what happened to those babies. There seemed to have been hundreds of them at the time but in thinking it over she says it was more likely ten, or maybe twenty. Whatever the number, their cries, and her helplessness haunted her, haunts her still.

They finally arrived at the town where Sary's mother had been born. Instead of the usual friendly respect, they were greeted by hostile villagers. The Khmer Rouge were very much in charge and the inhabitants were silent and subdued. All the houses in the village were closed to them, so they built themselves a temporary shelter under a tree. Sary's parents were so shattered by the forced move that they were unable to do more than sit speechless by the roadside, each being brave for the other. To them it must have seemed as though the Buddhist prophecy that darkness would descend and evil rule the world had come terrifyingly true. The grandfather's head and hands shook visibly. The grandmother never left his side, although she was never seen to touch him. Sary was now head of the family which at that point consisted of eleven people (her parents, sisters, six children and herself). Upon arrival they were immediately sent to register for work and from there directly to the paddy, even the bewildered grandparents and three-year-old Houssara. The cadres realized there was little to gain from the presence of the grandparents and they were set to carrying water instead of planting or digging ditches. Houssara was presented with a tiny hoe and encouraged to use it. This, they told him, is your proud new life, the future is yours. American oppression is over.

It was here that the now useless car and Samreth's bicycle were taken from them. It was here also that Sarin found them about a month or so later. Sarin's relief and joy at finding the family still alive can be imagined. The family who had almost given up hope of ever seeing him again greeted him with an enthusiasm that belied their dazed and weakened state. They all felt stronger in his presence. Sarin had taken some friends into South Vietnam thinking they would be safe where Son Ngoc Than was. He refused to stay with them. Sary was aghast; 'Why didn't you stay where you were safe?' she wanted to know. He told her he didn't want to live without her and the children.

Conversation was difficult, even the simplest kind. Khmer Rouge spies were everywhere and even the children were monitored. Children were used as informers, encouraged to report any incorrect remarks even from their own parents. Sary impressed on them all the need for secrecy, silence and discretion. When Sarin arrived in the village he was interrogated by the cadres now in charge. The family blessed his foresight in changing his clothes and burying his glasses which were a sure sign of a hated intellectual, but were terrified that one of the villagers would identify him. Either out of fear or gratitude for past kindnesses, no one came forward. During the interrogation Sary fainted, struck her head, and began bleeding. Instead of stopping the proceedings this only intensified the interrogation. No one offered to help her. When one of the cadres asked Sarin why a man in his position wasn't safely out of the country, Sarin answered, 'Since when was a farmer a man of position under Sihanouk?' Sarin seemed completely without fear and soon had his interrogators laughing. He was far too clever for these unschooled soldiers scarcely out of adolescence. It also taught Sary a lesson she was never to forget. No matter how terrified she was, she never again allowed her fear to show in front of any member of the Khmer Rouge.

Sary's mother was the first to die, which was unexpected. She was a vigorous woman, proud and erect and much younger than her husband. The Cambodian equivalent of a tomboy, she had married at fifteen. Her husband and her mother had to forbid her climbing trees during her first pregnancy. She, the ruling matriarch, terrified her sons, Sary's 'tall brothers' and intimidated even her husband. During her

94

middle years the mother became very religious and spent a great deal of time in the Pagoda. She ate sparingly and often fasted as Buddhist ritual required. Sary felt that the scarcity of food would bother her less than the others. Perhaps it did. It was the indignity, I think, more than anything else. The Khmer Rouge soon learned that there was little work to get out of her. They put it down to her age and her white hair. She and her whole generation were expendable and the sooner the better. She did what was required of her, slowly and silently, never raising her eyes to the guards. She never spoke. She used her silence as a weapon rather than a shield. She put aside some of her minuscule portion of rice for her husband who ate it as though under orders. The first satisfaction she showed was at Sarin's arrival. She had been waiting and praying for his return. She made the Buddhist gesture of bowed head and clasped hands and he knelt before her in tears. After a few weeks the grandmother died in her sleep. Sarin went to the 'leader' to report the death and was told that he could bury her after the day's work was over. Little did they know that this was a privilege. A privilege they would long for in the future and one that would not be repeated.

After a few months Sarin, Sary, her father and her two younger sisters as well as the six children were force-marched to a spot between Maung and Battambang in what became the Northwest Zone, fairly close to the border with Thailand. They were finally allowed to stop after what Kilen remembers as at least two months of walking and sleeping by the roadside. Along the way were derelict houses, empty and still, eerily quiet. Occasionally they saw some elderly people too weak or too ill to move who waved to them sadly. Only the very young cried, the others were stunned into silence. No one knew how long they walked: they walked until they were commanded to stop. No one knew which day it was. Each day was like the last, the commands were the same, the rations were the same, the misery was the same. When they finally stopped it was on a piece of land that was little more than a clearing in the jungle. There seemed to be hundreds of people already there living in makeshift shelters. Together with their group they were told they must build themselves a place to live. They arrived after dark and in the rain, only the cadres had shelter, they had none. Sary had wisely brought with her a mat made of plastic instead of the traditional straw. This kept the rain out. That night she and Sarin sat up holding the mat over the heads of the sleeping children. The next day Sarin felled some trees, stripped them for supports and collected palm leaves which Sary and the girls sewed together to make a roof. Sary found a piece of a wall from an abandoned bamboo shelter and dragged it back for their use. Despite all of Sarin's efforts the roof leaked and the wall of palm leaves shook in the wind. When the night rains were strong, they woke up drenched, the dirt floor turned into mud.

By this time their food supplies were exhausted and they were very hungry indeed. Samreth cut his leg which became swollen and badly infected and left him unable to walk. One morning he woke up to find the wound crawling with maggots: he screamed. The maggots, however, in eating away the putrefied flesh may well have prevented gangrene. Sarin went into the woods, found some leaves which he pounded into a thick paste and placed on the wound: it eventually healed. Poutherein had jaundice and was too weak to move. Kilen was the strongest of the children, and was able to help her parents. She went out every day with her father to look for roots or anything edible and she begged rice from the cadres. The place was vile as there was no sanitation, and the rains had churned the earth into a mass of mud and excrement. Diarrhea had afflicted almost everyone and many people were too weak to dig holes for their needs. Hunger drove people to desperate measures. Two young girls in a nearby shelter sat with their mother as she gave birth. When the baby was born they seized the placenta which they roasted and ate. The guards were shocked when they heard this and the two girls were taken away. The guards could afford to be 'shocked', their stomachs were full. The death rate rose alarmingly, and within about six or seven months the settlement had turned into a ghost town. The shelter closest to the Khuls had been filled with a large noisy family but it slowly became quieter and quieter until there was no one left. They never found out what happened to the bodies.

As she saw her siblings starving, Kilen became bold. Aged nine she went far afield to beg. This was against orders as any unauthorized movement was strictly forbidden. She even went as far as the town of Maung where the Khmer Rouge had their headquarters. Sometimes she was lucky and was given some rice and a few half-rotten vegetables from friendly soldiers. 'Please, sir, uncle,' she would say, 'can you give me some rice or some old vegetables?' Often she was chased away with nothing and once was given some roots but threatened with death if she returned. Once when questioned about her father, she lied and said he was a *cyclopousse* (a cycle-taxi driver). 'Your skin is too light' the soldiers said, 'your father must have been more important than a taxi-driver.' They laughed at her, gave her some rice and let her go. It was the small-grained variety that before the war was fed only to the pigs. But they gave her half a sackful and Kilen was grateful. She had to pass near a river that often had corpses in it floating downstream and one day she counted nine. She waded across this river almost every day. The most dangerous spot of all was the train station at Maung as it was always heavily guarded and no one was allowed near it. Kilen often had to pass it and she did so full

97

of fear, looking both ways and praying hard.

The family's need was so great and the excitement when she was successful so joyous that she kept going back for yet one more time. Until one dramatic day. She had asked some soldiers for permission to pick up wild fruit that had fallen from the trees. The permission had been granted but there was no fruit left. She was so worried that she failed to notice that a Khmer Rouge soldier had followed her on his bicycle. He stopped her as she neared a wood. She was with her younger brother, Noi, known in the family as Anut. The soldier promised to show Kilen where oranges grew wild in the woods. Noi was told to keep watch and warn them if anyone approached. She followed the soldier deeper and deeper into the woods. Finally he stopped but she saw no oranges. When he told her to lie down she knew she was in trouble and that something terrible could happen to her. She kicked him hard, screamed and ran away crying. As she reached Noi she called to him to start running, but Noi was so frightened that he was unable to move. Then another soldier who had heard her screams saw her and came over to ask what had happened. After she had sobbed out her story he shook her silent, made her promise not to tell anyone and gave her two Cambodian grapefruit. He grabbed hold of the soldier as he was coming out of the woods and began to beat him around the head. At the first sight of blood, Kilen and Noi began to run and ran all the way back to the family, carefully hugging the precious grapefruit (which Kilen assures me are much larger and sweeter than the Western kind). She told her parents what had happened. She had never seen her father cry before.

Noi became ill. He could no longer eat even the meagre rations that were available and then he was afflicted with diarrhea. The diarrhea increased in force accompanied by severe retching. The others worked all day and into the night while he lay alone in the shelter, sipping the herbal brew his father made for him that in spite of its increased bitterness did not stop the diarrhea. He grew thinner and thinner and his eight-year-old face became that of an old man. He asked to be taken to the hospital. Sary did her best to dissuade him. When he turned to her with bowed head, hands in the attitude of prayer, and said, 'Please, please, I don't want to die, I want to live,' she gave in. For three days they visited him in the hospital after working hours. On the fourth day Kilen was told that he had been transferred to Maung. They were not allowed to go to Maung, and never saw him again. They went on hoping that some news would come through, but after a few months they gave up hope and realized that he must be dead. Like other hospital dead he had probably been buried in a mass grave. They never learned where.

Sarin was ordered to leave the others and go to work on a construction site. He was forbidden to see his family or have any contact with them. He sometimes had news of them from friends or even more occasionally caught sight of one of them working in the fields. By 1975 American bombardments had almost completely destroyed Cambodian agriculture. This in a country where before the war almost ninety per cent of the population was dependent on agriculture. The Khmer Rouge set out to restore it, together with the canals and irrigation system vital to its development. In Cambodia control of the waters was essential as the monsoon, when it arrived, was very strong and lasted for only a short period. The new government demanded that over a million hectares of new fields be irrigated. That meant the construction of canals, dikes and dams. There were few tools and practically no technicians but there was an enormous supply of manpower. The Khmer Rouge took as its model the slave society of ancient Angkor. Under this system agriculture supported the cities and the Temples. The 1959 doctoral thesis of Khieu Sampan, one of their leaders, served as the Khmer Rouge Manifesto. In his thesis Khieu argued that the cities were parasitical and that Cambodia's strength and future lay in the development of the countryside. Cambodia, he wrote, should become industrialized but this could only happen if agriculture was developed first. An expanded and enlarged agriculture could in turn support industrialization and make Cambodia completely self-sufficient. This required almost complete mobilization of the country as a labour force. There were no arguments against this policy, no questions and no delay in its enforcement. Work on irrigation projects took place during the winter dry season, between the harvest and the early planting. For the remaining part of the year people worked in the fields and the countryside was covered with labourers – men, women and children. Currency was abolished together with the telephone and the postal system. The temple complex of Angkor Wat became the symbol of the revolution. Pictures of Pol Pot or Communist heroes were not displayed, only photographs or crude drawings of the temples.

Sarin was set to work constructing a dam. Sary volunteered to go into the fields for longer hours than required, hoping to spare her father labour she feared, rightly, would be too much for him. It was the beginning of the rainy season and by sheer good fortune she found a piece of nylon that protected her head as she worked. She was allowed to take her elder daughter, Poutherein, with her. Samreth had been sent to work in another paddy with boys his own age. When Sary first began to work the nylon proved invaluable but when the rains grew stronger and the mud became gummy it was of less use. Walking, even lifting one's foot was a problem, but they kept at it doggedly. Sary was ingenious when the break for midday rice came. She built a small mud fort around herself, put Poutherein on her lap, covered her head with the precious nylon and, miraculously, they slept.

As soon as a child was six family life completely ceased and he was taken to a work camp where he lived with other children his age. There were to be no blood ties in the New World, family names and terms of endearment were outlawed, too. Everyone was addressed as *Mit bong* (comrade), literally comrade older brother. Samreth as the eldest was taken away first. Then Poutherein. She went with her aunts – Sary's sisters – to a women's camp. She was tall for her age and hoped to be allowed to stay as she had heard the food was better and more plentiful than in the children's camps. It was – but the work, digging canals out of land as hard as rock, was backbreaking. Her aunts were strong young women in their twenties, she was not yet twelve. Desperate, she ran away to join her father on the dam construction site. She was caught and sent back to her camp. By this time she was so weak that the only job the 'leader' felt she was capable of was watching and feeding the chickens and ducks (supplying food for the cadres). She lived in the chicken coop and thought herself very fortunate. The only drawback was the chicken fleas: she scratched and scratched knowing she must pay something for this cushy job. She could also eat some of the ducks' food, another bonus. She drew what water there was from a stagnant puddle at the back of the chicken coop, which was also the watering place of the cows who slopped in the mud there. At first she was afraid to drink the water, it was so dirty, but then she realized she would soon die of thirst without it. Once a week they were allowed to go to the river. It took most of the day as it was miles away down a steep canyon. It was a beautiful walk down through fields of wild flowers and lush undergrowth: the walk back was hellish.

Sary had been left behind with the two youngest children and her dying father. One day she almost lost her youngest daughter, Puit. The child saw a small sack of salt lying, unclaimed, on the path near their shelter. It had undoubtedly been dropped by accident and it seemed to belong to no one so the five-year-old girl picked it up to take to her mother. A Khmer Rouge guard saw her, grabbed her by the hair and dragged her into Sary's shelter as the evening meal was being prepared. The soldier announced that this pale, trembling child was a thief: A thief! The grandfather staggered to his feet to protect the girl and screamed abuse at the soldier but Sary was too quick-witted for them all. She pushed her father aside and slapped the little girl's face. 'How dare you?' she said, 'After all the *Angka* has done for you? How could you become a thief when the *Angka* loves you, protects you from the Americans, shame, shame!' She promised she would deal with the child and deal harshly. The soldier went away satisfied. Only then did the shaking child and the grandfather began to sob. Sary comforted them as best she could.

Both Sary and Sarin believed that the grandfather would not last long after his wife's death. They were wrong. Some of the grandmother's strength seemed to pass on to him. This spare, elegant man continued to carry water and do the most humble tasks assigned to him, solemn and dignified as though he was still running the National Post Office. His tremors persisted but did not noticeably increase and he was even able to make the long, painful forced march to the new settlement. When they finally arrived, in the rain, they found one of his old friends who had a small place in his shelter. The friend took him in until Sarin was able to complete the family 'home'. The grandfather was invaluable when Poutherein contracted jaundice and Samreth hurt his leg: telling stories, cheering the children, singing songs and changing dressings on Samreth's wound. Since his work kept him nearer to the shelter than the others, he was Noi's closest companion during his fatal illness. He began to decline when Sarin was sent away, but he kept to his assigned tasks. As each child was taken away he became more and more childlike himself. After the episode with Puit and the salt he was lucid as he told Sary that her quick thinking had saved the child, but he never spoke intelligibly after that. Then Puit was sent to a children's camp and he was alone with Sary and Houssara. One day he collapsed while he was carrying water to the workers in the paddy fields. No one picked up the body (which may or may not have had life left in it) until the day's work was over. By that time he was certainly dead. When Sary heard about it, the body had been taken away with two others, who had died the day before in the neighbouring paddy. Sary heard no more.

A new 'leader' was appointed to Sary's section. She had seen him before and knew immediately she had somehow offended him. She trembled for them all. His name was Chac and he was a square-faced, shrill-voiced man of indeterminate age. He was, however, a firm believer in Khmer Rouge doctrine, which he followed assiduously. He singled Sary out but in order to punish her he must first catch her in error. The easiest way to catch a woman, Sary said, was to appoint her to be a cook for the cadres. Hunger was such that nearly all the cooks at one time or another took a piece of food from the cooking pot: a serious crime. Sary was aware of this and aware of the constant spying. She never took so much as a spoonful of soup, she did no 'wrong doing' and Chac's plan failed. She was soon sent back to the fields.

Later, after the grandfather's death, she heard through friends that a guard had tried to poison Sarin. Sarin suspected what had happened and knew the antidote. He was very ill, so ill that he was allowed to send for Sary. She asked Chac for permission to see her husband one more time. Fortunately, the rules allowed this and after a full day's work she walked the several hours to Sarin's camp arriving just before dawn. She shook the dust from her clothes, smoothed her hair and hid her fears as best she could. Then she went directly to the 'leader'. 'Why?' she demanded, 'do you want to kill my husband? Tell me, comrade, has he done anything wrong, was he not good?' The 'leader' denied all knowledge of the attempt and promised to help them. He did. He allowed Sary and Houssara to come to live in Sarin's camp. It was a brave and generous act. The Khmer Rouge had divided the country into geographical zones, then into regions (*dambans*), then into districts (*srok*) and finally into sub-districts (*khum*). Fortunately Sarin's 'leader' had a *srok* and Chac merely a *khum* so he was overruled.

At that time things had eased a bit and they were given a small piece of land (about ten square metres) that could be cultivated for their own use. They grew some corn. Sarin insisted that they share their produce with the others. When Sary objected that they were too hungry to be so generous, he told her that others were just as hungry and that if they did not help they would soon have no neighbours. After a few months a new 'leader' was appointed and Sary and Houssara were sent away. A year or so later Sary learned that the first (kindly) 'leader' had been executed together with his entire family. They never learned the reason. Within their communes the power of the 'leaders' was absolute – while it lasted. They, too, were subject to the abrupt changes and power struggles within the *Angka*.

Rumours of political upheavals circulated throughout the camps. The only reliable proof of any rumour was the easing, or increasing, of the work load, or a change in the food supply. In August 1975 it was announced that currency was going to be re-introduced. There were continual rumours regarding the struggles within the Khmer Rouge between the so-called moderates from the zone east of the

Mekong against the more radicalized Chinese-orientated cadres from the Southwest. The North and Northwest zones seemed to be in conflict with the rulers in Phnom Penh over the suppression of all personal freedom. A slight improvement in late 1975 and early 1976 was quickly and completely reversed with the ascendancy of Pol Pot over his rivals and the elimination of anyone who questioned his authority. Chances for whatever freedom of choice that might have come with the re-introduction of money vanished. The food supply around Maung, where the family was, grew especially scarce in late 1976 and 1977. Sarin was still working at the dam site. Kilen, 'Daddy's girl' once caught sight of him as she was being marched to her own place of labour. Seeing her father with a beard, a headscarf and a loin cloth was a shock. The girls were singing as they marched (Kilen says they always had to sing when there was anyone around) and she sang extra loud hoping he would recognize her voice. He did not look up and she was afraid to call out to him. Mercifully, she did not know that this was to be her last glimpse of him.

Houssara was only three when the Khmer Rouge came to power so his recollections were far more limited than those of the older children. Khmer Rouge policy was to place children in camps for what was called political education, and was in reality brainwashing, indoctrination and hard labour in the rice paddy or on construction sites. One by one Sary's remaining children were taken away. Houssara, being the youngest (his family name is Pul which means 'the last') was the only child left with her in 1977. They were both starving. Houssara said to his mother, she tells me: 'Ma, the next time the soldiers come around tell them I am six. That way they will take me away and we'll both have more to eat.' He was five. He was taken to the children's camp and Sary found herself alone for the first time in her life. Houssara's bravery and generosity were conquered by loneliness and fright and he came running back to Sary. She was terrified, fully aware of the penalty for breaking 'the rules'. She immediately took him back to 'the leader', emphasizing the child's desire to go to the camp sooner than his actual age permitted, and promising it would not happen again. A few weeks later she found him once again curled up on her floor. This time she was even more frightened. 'He'll kill you' she said and when this seemed to make little difference to an exhausted, battered five-year-old she tried, 'He'll kill me, too'. This had more effect and they managed to sneak him back into camp before he was missed. When he made his third escape, she completely lost control. She began shaking violently, her eyes rolled back in her head until only the whites showed and the terrorized child realized for the first time the enormity of what he had done. Sary fed him her week's supply of rice and the two of them made their way back to the children's camp. The path led along a deep canal and at one point Sary said, 'If you ever run away again they will kill not just you and me but Samreth, Poutherein, Kilen and Puit as well. I don't want to live without my children so I'll throw myself in the canal now. It is far better than seeing my children die.' Houssara fell on his knees in front of her, begged for forgiveness and swore never to run away again. He never did.

By this time a new ruling had set up communal kitchens and no 'private' food was allowed. Anything that could be scavenged or found in the woods had to be carefully hidden. In many camps the punishment for hiding food was stoning, usually to death. This ruling with its baleful punishment intimidated most people but not Samreth. He and one of his friends managed to catch two fish when they were bathing in the river, somehow catching them in their hands. Samreth wanted to keep them alive as long as possible but the danger of discovery was too great. The boys hid their catch in their shirts and the fish stayed cool for the long walk back to camp. Once there the problem was how to hide the precious catch and what to do with it. The traditional methods of preserving fish were out of the question – there was no salt and drying in the sun took too long and was too smelly. They tried edging up to the camp fire and thrust one fish into the embers but it had to be retrieved before it was anywhere near cooked. If the Japanese eat raw fish, why can't we, they decided. Where and how they were to be eaten was the next and perhaps most serious of all their problems. In the camp Samreth was known for his prowess in climbing trees so no one thought it strange when he tried the tallest one around (till then unclimbed) and with a certain effort made it to the very top. He was cheered by some of his fellows who had no idea that he was there to hide his raw and half-cooked fish. The catch was safe and for the next two nights Samreth and his friend (who was on a lower branch) had a tree feast. Never had anything tasted so wonderful! Not everyone in the family however was so fortunate or so enterprising. Poutherein was once reduced to eating raw snails and Sarin to eating raw worms retrieved from a cow pat.

Sarin became ill from overwork and harsh treatment. He was taunted at the site as the 'American' or the 'Great Senator' and given the most arduous and humiliating jobs. He was kicked and beaten if he staggered or fell. He grew weaker and weaker and finally succumbed to high fever and delirium. Eventually he became so ill that he was sent back to Sary. He was ordered to go to the hospital. At first he refused. Despite his pleas, or perhaps because of them, he was taken forcibly to the local hospital. There was no medicine available so Sary boiled a root to make a brew capable, she believed, of bringing down even the highest fever. She took it to the hospital hoping to give it to him. Both she and

Sarin were convinced, and, tragically, they were right, that this hospital was a sort of clearing house where the unwanted died without too much fuss or outside knowledge. She was not permitted entry but an old friend whose services as a doctor were still needed by the Khmer Rouge saw her, took the brew and pleaded with her to leave at once and not come back. The visit did not go unobserved and the next day Sary was sent to work far away, too far to walk to the hospital. She learned through the doctor how Sarin died; his guard had injected air into his veins to economize on bullets. 'He knew his end was near,' said the doctor and sent loving messages to them all. As soon as she heard the news Sary went back to the hospital and asked the 'leader' if she might have his body for proper burial. 'No need' she was told, the *Angka* had taken care of everything for her.

At Khao-I-Dang she met the doctor's daughter who confirmed the story and added that her own father had survived for only a short time afterwards. When Sarin died Sary was surprised at the extent of genuine mourning. Where so many died daily mourning had become a luxury, grief an extra burden. Sarin's kindness had not gone unnoticed. He had drained himself in the service of his fellow victims. Often he had stayed awake at night when it rained filling the earthen water jugs for his neighbours to spare them a trip to the river. Exhausted by a long day's labour most people slept through the night rains and failed to fill their water pots. Sarin did it for them, saving them a long and difficult walk. When he had food he shared it, when children were ill he found herbal medicines for them, when the elderly grew weak he sat with them and cheered them as best he could. His teaching skills were helpful, too. There were several ethnic Chinese who scarcely knew how to speak Khmer. Under the zenophobic Khmer Rouge regime it was a serious offense to utter any words that were not Khmer. Sarin held secret classes for them at night. Several old people came to Sary surreptitiously in tears: weeping for the dead was not permitted in the new order. These elderly people bewailed their lost 'son' as they called Sarin, lamenting that it was he and not they who had died.

Although she was unable to save her parents or her husband, Sary did manage to rescue some of her children. Her courage and quick thinking saved Samreth's life. He had been caught by a Khmer Rouge soldier stealing a piece of fruit. He had been condemned. First of all he was forced to dig his own grave as per the *Angka* custom, then tied to a tree with a bunch of mangoes just out of reach and left to sit in the sun. He was very, very hungry. The soldiers brought his mother to see his disgrace. Instead of weeping and begging to have him released, she sized up the situation at a glance and began to scream: 'If my son is a traitor to the people and steals their food, he should be punished, punish him as you like, I want to see his evil blood flow.' The soldiers were so impressed that after a severe warning to Samreth they let him go. He had been tied up without food or water for over ten hours. Samreth was terrified by his mother's performance believing it to be her true feeling. Their camps were close enough for him to visit her occasionally. After this he did not come near her for over three months. One day Sary saw Samreth running past her shelter and she ran after him and grabbed him. Samreth was terrified, fell to his knees and begged his mother not to hurt him. He was too young to understand what had happened. The loss of his mother was to him more dreadful than any threat of the Khmer Rouge. Sary held the shaking boy tightly as she explained. To ask for kindness or sympathy from the Khmer Rouge, she told him, only made them more brutal, she knew it was useless to plead with them. Samreth understood that she had been pretending in order to save his life and thanked her. They both hugged and cried. Samreth, afterwards, visited his mother whenever it was permitted.

Months later Houssara became very ill. He was taken from his camp to the hospital where Sary went to visit him. He had been placed in the ward with the dying. He was hemorrhaging internally and blood dripped continually from his rectum. Knowing hospital conditions and seeing that Houssara had already been placed with the dying, Sary went to her group 'leader'. She told him her youngest son was dying and asked that she be allowed to take him into her shelter. She explained calmly that no extra ration of rice would be necessary and that she would gather leaves and roots in the woods to make medicines for the child. The 'leader' looked at her carefully and asked, 'Are you a doctor?' 'I am not a doctor,' she told him, 'I am a mother and I know that my son's case is hopeless.' She went on to say 'If the Angka does not want me to bring my son back to die, well that is alright, too, but I feel I must try.' She asked him if he would be willing to let his own child die in the hands of the Angka, and that if he could, so could she. He said certainly he would be willing. The reply unnerved her, but not for long. She rose to her feet and burst into laughter that gradually became hysterical. When the 'leader' wanted to know why she was laughing she told him she was content, even happy, as she had done all she could for her son and she need feel no guilt. The Angka had decreed that her son should be left to die in the hospital, so be it. She never found out exactly what it was that made the 'leader' change his mind, but she was given the permission she craved. She went to the hospital, put the emaciated, bleeding body of Houssara in a piece of cloth and carried him 'home'. Every day from then on, before she left for the fields, she filled an iron cooking pot with sand covered with water and placed this on the child's stomach to cool it. After about five days the bleeding stopped. Houssara was a survivor by vocation. After the bleeding stopped, little by little Houssara began to grow stronger. Soon he was strong enough to be taken back to his camp where he stayed until the Vietnamese arrived some six or seven months later.

Khmer Rouge policy to separate families and place all children in camps according to their age and sex was to create the new people, the pure, the perfect people, the true sons and daughters of the Khmer Rouge, free from any outside influence. There was an almost mystical belief in the possibility of perfection, with an elaborate set of rules to be followed. These rules seemed to possess a horrible clarity unhampered by judgment or experience. When the regime's unrealizable economic goals failed to materialize its leaders claimed the rules had not been observed and enemies within were blamed. Violence and terror were institutionalized to protect the revolution and to lead the way to perfection. Absolute loyalty to the new government was demanded. Most revolutions recruit among the young: there is a strong appeal, the promise of the future, the excitement. The Khmer Rouge went further, they used the young as a basis for their revolution. Children were encouraged to spy on one another and on their parents. Some soldiers had run away from home at twelve years old: the Party became their family. No one received a formal education, they were indoctrinated, trained to obey rather like a prized animal. On command they ran, clear-eyed, into battle. Complete domination over the country gave the Khmer Rouge the opportunity to put their wild, pseudo-scientific theories into practice. The seemingly endless supply of guinea pigs kept the practice going as they continued to try out their ideas.

When Kilen was taken off to the children's work camp she was wise enough, even at ten, to hide her beauty. Her memory of the attempted rape was vivid. She smeared mud on her face, never tidied her hair and mumbled disjointed sentences when spoken to. All this primarily to escape the unwanted attentions of the camp guards. 'I didn't want to be where I was or who I was,' she said. She created a strange other child, like the imaginary friend of a lonely childhood. This was originally for her own safety but later became something more. Slowly this creature developed a life of her own and Kilen found herself being the protector for this poor 'wanting' girl no older than herself and the roles were reversed. The camps were, from Kilen's description, a combination of daily drudgery and distrust: cruel and terribly isolating. I have often wondered how this collective madness affected them. After all, it lasted for over four years. Within such a system it was impossible for a child to feel the uniqueness, importance and individuality so necessary for his development. How could any child trust or believe in anyone or anything that made him feel so unimportant?

On arrival the children's clothes were taken from them and they were dressed in black: there was a choice between trousers or a skirt. Kilen chose a skirt because she felt holes wouldn't show up so clearly and in the vain hope that she might hide some food under it. Each child was issued with a spoon, a hoe and a sickle and told that they must be carefully guarded as they could not be replaced and if lost or broken the child must hoe, cut and eat with her hands. Kilen hid her spoon and slept with her feet on her sickle and her arms around her hoe. They were also given a rag (like the traditional *kromah*) that was to serve as headgear, towel, handkerchief or anything else. These were their possessions; they never saw their shoes again. The boys and girls were separated as were any family members. At one point Kilen and Poutherein found themselves in the same camp: a comfort to them both. No one knew that they were sisters. They developed a language and a series of signs that the others could not understand, an essential precaution because the rules forbade certain conversations and any show of emotion or affection was severely punished. Their 'language' consisted mostly of signs and sounds of sorrow – they developed an algebra of their own against the arithmetic of others.

Poutherein was so weak from continual illness that she could hardly work but Kilen was able to help her fill her work quotas. This did not escape the notice of the spies. Poutherein was subjected to criticism and the sisters were terrified. Twice she was singled out by one of the other girls and reported to the leaders. With the cruelty of the miserable the other girls chose to torment Poutherein sensing her weakness. One night in the shelter she completely lost control and screamed at the other girls calling them animals. She still remembers the relief she felt after her outburst, all possible danger forgotten. At least she was still a person with feelings, a person who could make her presence felt to others, even if in a negative, painful way. Kilen begged her to stop, telling her she would get the whole family killed. Neither of them slept that night, certain it would be their last. They hugged each other, they cried silently, they sat together and waited for daybreak. Strangely, nothing was reported: they never understood why but were thankful. Not long afterwards Poutherein was sent to another camp, a camp for older children. They were almost relieved when she was transferred. It was hard not to say a proper farewell to each other, tears were forbidden and it would be as dangerous as talking about the good food they had eaten in the past. Their 'language' helped.

In Kilen's camp the children slept on the ground on thin mats, their only shelter a thatched roof supported by four tree trunks stripped clean in spots. Amazingly the roof let in practically no rain but during a storm all the children had to sleep in the very middle as the sides were open. Kilen talked little to her fellow victims, even at that age there were spies among them, making friends could be dangerous. The work load was so heavy that the girls, aged between ten and twelve, had little strength left for chat. The silence in the shelter was broken only by the sounds of weeping children or the shrieks of nightmares. Awakened at dawn, given a bowl of watery rice, the children were taken to the rice paddy for a day's work that lasted until nightfall. There was a break in the middle of the day with more soup eaten in the paddy where they tried to catch a bit of rest. The food was sparse but enough to sustain life. What was torture was the lack of sufficient water. Kilen said she often squeezed what she could from the mud in the rice paddy, or if possible drank the water remaining in a footprint or better still, hoof print where the ground had been pressed down. A meager supper at night and then, what they dreaded most, political indoctrination. For Kilen the most miserable part of a miserable day. The children, some sixty or seventy in each camp with guards and bosses, or as Kilen called them, 'Pol Pots', bringing the total to almost a hundred, sat cross-legged on the ground forming a circle, the camp's bosses in the center close to the fire. The children huddled together for warmth and to support the bodies of the most exhausted. They were congratulated on their great good fortune as chosen daughters of the Khmer Rouge and they cheered and sang in their poor cracked voices. The compliments did not apply to them all: the guards would often single out a child who would be made to stand and bear criticism. Usually the charge was lingering at her work. The child was made to apologize and all the others clapped and chanted a number. The numbers were terrifying because three complaints signi- fied disappearance and no one was naïve enough not to realize what that meant. Kilen was forced to clap but only mouthed the number. When it was 'three' the guilty child took her place on the ground in silence and even the guards were still for a while. One dreadful night a child was singled out for stealing an orange. 'What shall we do to her?' screamed the guards. The children screamed, 'Orange soil, orange soil . . .' This time Kilen screamed with them as the guards were especially menacing. The child's death was inevitable so what could they do but play to their tormentors? The killings took place out of eyesight but not out of hearing and the sounds haunt Kilen still: 'That sound weighs on my heart,' she says.

Fragile and delicate as she looked Kilen was a strong and productive worker. She was 'promoted' to a First Line camp after about a year. The routine was the same only the food was better and a bit more plentiful. This unfortunately did not last long and Kilen was sent to Bung Trou Yun in the mountains where conditions were harsher than ever, so harsh that she became very ill. She was sent back and then to the hospital. In the hospital she was surrounded by death – very few patients survived their stay. There were no medicines and coconut juice was used to cure everything. Most of the 'doctors' and 'nurses' could barely read or write. The only advantage was that one was not forced to work. This, for someone as weak and ill as Kilen, was blessing enough. There was an old woman in the bed next to hers who was dying of dysentery. 'Just like my little brother,' thought Kilen. No one had come near the old woman except to cut a hole in the bed for the continual flux. Her uneaten food was not taken away and it attracted flies and ants. The stench was unbearable. Weak as she was herself Kilen tried to keep the flies away and to keep from retching as she washed the old lady every day. She crawled to the river nearby to wash her filthy clothes and she changed the old lady as if she were her infant. She held her hand as she died.

Kilen grew stronger and was discharged from the hospital and sent back to the 'First Line'. On her way there she ran into Poutherein who was being sent, together with her entire camp, to Bung Trou Yun, the fearsome camp in the mountains. Kilen was aghast as Poutherein was still very weak. She warned her sister of the dreadful conditions of the place and so frightened her that Poutherein determined not to go. Together with several others she hid when the members of the camp were rounded up for transfer. They could not escape notice for long and one by one they were all caught. They were herded together and closed in a sealed compound all day. When night came they were taken outside to a clearing among banana trees and seated in a circle around three heavily armed 'leaders'. The slight moon had just begun to rise, the sky was dark and immense. The shadows of the trees made a confining wall that seemed to move closer and closer. Although the night air was warm Poutherein shivered, her body covered with the sweat of fear. One of the 'leaders' had a flashlight – a wonder in itself. He flashed the light on their faces one at a time. Each thought it a signal of death to come. There were three men among the dozen or so women. Each man was called to the center and beaten badly with rifle butts. Two of the men were stoic and only grunted under the blows. The third begged his tormentors to stop, promising to do anything they wanted. It was this luckless third who was taken into the banana grove by one of the armed men. The terrified group heard pleas, screams and then silence. The cadre emerged, his bayonet still bloody. The rest were told that their lives would be spared but that they must leave for Bung Trou Yun the next morning. They all agreed as though it were a treat: at least they were alive.

They were on their way at dawn as it was a six-day walk. They never arrived. The Vietnamese had invaded and all order broke down. Kilen was vague about time, understand-

ably so. No one had a watch, even the guards had little artificial light and only the sun could be relied upon. When the
day was sunny, four large steps from one's shadow signified
nine o'clock but often they forgot to measure. Time was
reckoned by the cultivation of rice: the planting, weeding
and harvesting delineated the year more clearly than any cal-
endar. The routine was dreary and exhausting but in a way,
welcomed: she felt safer in the paddy, Kilen said. There was
neither time nor wish for the new and exciting experiences
that most children love, expectations were few and pleasure
completely absent. Four and a half years taken from a childhood is an eternity.

PART IV

They have found out: it is hard to escape from Cambodia,
   Hard to escape the justice of Pol Pot,
When they are called to report in dreams to their tormentors.
   One night is merciful, the next is not.

I hear a child moan in the next room and I see
   The nightmare spread like rain across his face
And his limbs twitch in some vestigial combat
   In some remembered place.

I WANTED TO HEAR their stories in a more complete form
than the bits and pieces that popped out from time to time.
For example, when we bought Houssara a bicycle Samreth
was reminded of how he had loaded his own with food when
he was forced out of Phnom Penh, but here he stopped.

What follows is what I have managed to piece together.
Getting complete stories was not easy. Sary is confused and
the language presents a problem with her, although she is a
wonderful actress and has shown me a great deal. Houssara
really remembers little or nothing. Kilen, even now after all
these years, breaks down and weeps so I haven't the heart to
ask her too much. That leaves Samreth and Poutherein. They
are both articulate, Samreth in broken Italian (strangely
after all these years he insists in speaking Italian to myself
and John) and Poutherein in fairly good but breathless
English. Samreth's story is confused and at times incoherent
but rings terrifyingly true. He tells it with intervals of
Oriental laughter and with his usual charm. From time to
time he says, as he often does 'Cosa potevo fare' or 'perché'
(what could I do or why?), as if someone could supply an
answer. Poutherein is more self-conscious, her story more
organized, her phrasing unique and her acting superb.
'Thank God I was born in a politic family', she says, 'I look
those guys in the eye and tell them what they want to hear.'
This for anyone from a Khmer Rouge cadre to a Red Cross
worker or an American immigration official.

The children were all lovers of truth but in Samreth it was

an obsession. I remember when he first began to understand Italian television. 'Is it true,' he asked, 'that if I eat my *merenda* I will become stronger and wiser?' I explained as best I could that he was watching *pubblicità* (a commercial) and that it was not necessarily 'true'. He was disgusted. What was the point, he wondered, of lying when your life didn't depend on it? When bit by bit he began his story I knew that, although disjointed and sometimes scarcely understandable, it would be 'true'.

When the family was forced out of Phnom Penh into the country, shortly after the Khmer Rouge victory, Samreth was sent to work in the fields. His independent spirit caused him trouble there but his mother's proximity and his own sense of survival kept him going. Early on the 'leaders' in the work camps were benign, almost. They were young, unschooled boys and girls who had spent several miserable years in the jungle and were tasting power for the first time. The degree of power they held corrupted rapidly and the humane were soon replaced. Part of the cadres' duty was to instruct the 'new people' and inform them of the advantages that were to be theirs under the new system, as well as the dangers for those who did not conform. This was called 'political education'. At first there was little of this as teenage semi-literate boys and girls have little to say. Bit by bit they developed their own brand of jargon, a language of their own. Samreth hated it. 'Why,' he asked, 'couldn't they talk like everyone else?' I often wondered if Samreth's disdain for language, any language, didn't come from this period in his life. 'Sorry' was abolished as was 'please'. 'You couldn't be sorry,' said Samreth, 'or sick'. Punishment was announced in jargon as was the rare praise. 'You are responsible for your own safety' was a favorite phrase. What it actually meant, says Samreth, was 'if you don't do as you are ordered, anything can, and probably will, happen to you.' What they all dreaded most was to hear one of the 'leaders' say, 'You're history', or the phrase 'To keep you is no profit, to lose you, no loss'. Everyone knew those phrases meant death.

After some time (he has no idea how long it actually was) he was moved into a group called 'Front Line', and sent about 150 kilometers from his family. He is vague about the location but insists on the distance. 'Front line?' I asked. 'Did that mean they gave you a gun?' 'No, no, they didn't give me a gun until the Vietnamese came.'

Whether it was a spirit of adventure or that he was unaware of the extent of the Khmer Rouge madness and the danger it implied, I don't know, but he ran away and decided he would set out on his own. He was small for his age which was about eleven or twelve, slim, and very beautiful. He was able to slip into, and fortunately, out of, all manner of situations. He was wise with the wisdom of necessity, and sought some form of protection as soon as possible. As he was walking along the road he came upon a family composed entirely of women (mother, grandmother and daughter) and offered his services. They were on their way to try to find the mother's husband, an important general. Samreth knew he was important because they had four cows (I assume he meant bullocks or oxen but he insisted on calling them cows): two pulling their cart and two tied behind – unheard-of wealth. They also had a hidden store of gold and diamonds but it was the cows that held the real value. This 'important' family, like so many other Cambodians, was involved with both sides, or more correctly, all sides, in the conflict. The war in Cambodia was indeed a family affair: Sihanouk had fought his cousin Prince Sirik Matak (an ally of Lon Nol); Matak's brother Prince Sisowath Méthavi went into exile in Peking with Sihanouk; Pol Pot fought against his own brother. The family's grandmother spoke Thai and Vietnamese and worked secretly for the Khmer Rouge while the mother's husband was a general with Lon Nol. Samreth's protection only lasted a short while before the Khmer Rouge reclaimed him and took him into the mountains. He was told that he was near the frontier with Laos. We assume that he was somewhere in the Dangrek Mountain range. Conditions were even harsher than before, the food more scarce. Each soldier had a tube of material, about the size of a shirt sleeve, knotted at both ends. This was filled with rice and worn about the neck and from it a daily ration of rice was taken. To Samreth it was incredible how long one of these sleeves could last, ten days for each sleeve and some of the soldiers had four or five slung about their necks. Samreth, even today, admires the discipline and dedication of these Khmer Rouge cadres, who, hungry as they were, rationed themselves with rice. 'That's why they won the war,' he says. The workers were not entrusted with a sleeve. They were fed rice once a day and potato once a week. Water had to be scrounged from the earth, unless they were fortunate enough to be working near a stream. Samreth was disorientated and unsure of where he was – the Khmer Rouge may have lied to him about his whereabouts to discourage escape. He remembers the back-breaking work of digging a canal out of the mountainside, his perpetual hunger and little else. Although slightly built Samreth has extraordinary strength which he undoubtedly owes to the Khmer Rouge. He also owes them a pair of bandy legs, a product of an overworked, underfed body and a crooked hand, broken when smashed by a rifle butt.

One day the camp was in turmoil, the leaders stopped work and held what seemed to be non-stop meetings. Among the workers, speculation ran high. There were new fears, but the respite from labour was so welcome that they revelled in the unexpected holiday. The workers were assembled and the leaders announced the incursion of the Vietnamese into Cambodia. The meetings had been held to determine future action and it was decided to go deeper into the mountains and build a defense against the invader. The workers were told to prepare to leave camp, nothing else. They were given no indication that the Vietnamese were close by. No one doubted that there was something being planned, but what? They had always gone to work at daybreak and so when they left the camp well past sun-up they were certain something unusual was happening. The unconcealed anxiety of his leaders gave Samreth a particular happiness. They were marched along a river where they were allowed to drink. There were fish in the river, but they were not allowed to catch them. Although the workers were starving and the cadres themselves were hungry, Khmer Rouge rules decreed that if everyone did not fish, no one could. Samreth was once called 'an American' even for asking if he might try to catch some, obviously the lowest form of insult.

As they were marching they heard shots apparently from the approaching Vietnamese. Then, as though by a miracle, a gift of Buddha, Samreth saw a chicken (where it came from he is still uncertain, but there it was) and he refused to go any further. The 'leaders' ordered him to hurry but he refused to obey. 'I'm not going' he said, 'I'm going to eat that chicken.' His leaders were insistent but in such a rush that they left him there swearing to come back and kill him. They obviously did not want to risk revealing their whereabouts with a gunshot then. Samreth does not remember if he figured this out at the time. Nothing mattered any longer. The hope, the chance, the blessed possibility of eating a chicken was the most important thing to a starving boy. He felt strangely free, and no longer afraid in spite of the threats and the sound of approaching gunfire. It felt wonderful to be no longer doing what everyone else was doing, or thinking what they were thinking or eating what they were eating. I found Samreth's spontaneous use of the word 'freedom' interesting under the circumstances: freedom being defined by what one has at the moment. Samreth took a piece of wood and killed the chicken, made a fire to cook it and watched with glee as the 'Pol Pots' fled into the mountains. Still unafraid and gloriously full he was just finishing off the chicken when the Vietnamese soldiers arrived. 'What are you doing, little boy?' they asked in Cambodian. 'Finishing my chicken', he told them, innocently. They were dressed like the Khmer Rouge, although their uniforms were dark grey instead of black, but they were armed with the same guns so when one of the soldiers spoke to him in his own language, he was frightened. Bewildered and confused, he feared a Khmer Rouge trick. He knew he could not try an escape and at that moment he thought himself 'dead, my soul had already gone'. He was reassured when he heard them speaking Vietnamese among themselves. Anything, anything at all, would be better than falling into the hands of the Khmer Rouge again.

The Vietnamese said, 'Come along with us, little boy, it is dangerous here'. So he went with them. 'No one cares what you think, just what you do.' He went with them back to Battambang. Following this move his story becomes confused, and he tells it in a series of disjointed images. Samreth found himself at the train station in Battambang: a train loaded with guns was expected to arrive from Phnom Penh. At the time the city of Battambang was divided between the Khmer Rouge and the Vietnamese. He had been lured back to the Khmer Rouge. (Whether the Vietnamese no longer needed his services or if he left them, I don't know and he is not certain that he remembers.) They played 'love music' (Cambodian pop music, which he says he never liked before) from the old times and promised him that he could go back to the 'old ways', that he could even join his family again. And in his desperate need to believe them, he slipped away and went back.

That is where and when he was given a gun of his own. What they didn't tell him was that the Vietnamese were waiting for the train, too. 'Let us get a gun and kill Vietnamese,' they said and Samreth had the excitement of firing several rounds of ammunition. There were Khmer Rouge on one side of the train, Vietnamese on the other, all dressed and armed in the same manner. Samreth, unknowingly, went towards them to shake hands only to hear them speak Vietnamese. 'Totum tutum totum' went the guns on both sides with a dazed boy in the middle. 'No one knew who was who or what was what,' he said. On one side of the train he saw Khmer Rouge dead and dying: the others had fled. The Vietnamese let him go. His gun was without ammunition so useless now, but they took it anyway. His military career, brief and inglorious, was over. He took to the road again.

In the confusion that followed the fall of Battambang to the Vietnamese, the Khmer Rouge were among the refugees trying to get to the border camps. 'Were they running from the Vietnamese?' I asked. Samreth thought most of them were running from the 'Pol Pots' whom they no longer wanted to follow. Some of the cadres were recognized by the other refugees. 'That one killed my brother,' screamed a woman and one luckless man was knifed to death in front of Samreth. Others were beaten by furious, victimized Cambodians. Samreth recognized one of the cadres who had treated him badly but he said nothing, secretly pleased that he could still feel an 'old feeling' and not give in to brutality. The mayhem continued and Samreth's laugh grew hysterical as he described how ears were cut off, beatings administered and the remaining 'Pol Pots' ran away amid the jeers of their erstwhile victims.

Listening to the children's accounts of the horrors I realized that this was the only time any of them actually saw a killing. Reading other accounts, I find the same thing. There were many dead and dying but the killings took place out of sight. Not out of hearing. So consistent were these reports that it seems to me to be a definite Khmer Rouge policy decision. I have wondered myself, and asked others, why the killings always took place out of sight. Secrecy and mystery are often associated with tyranny, but this sort of semi-secrecy has always puzzled me. Other accounts I have read also mention this. As far as I know none of the refugees actually saw a Khmer Rouge execution although many claim to have seen the bodies of the victims. No one I have asked has either an answer or a theory. The closest to an explanation (for me) comes from a poem by Norman Cameron. Satan finding a rebel devises a horrible punishment and places a vitriol-soaked mask on his face: 'The renegade begins to scream with pain/(The mask is not designed to gag the sound,/which propagates the terror of his reign.) There is still more./Yet Satan has a stronger hold: the fear/That, if his rule is threatened, he will tear/The mask from that pain-crazed automaton/And show his vassals just what he has done.'

On the road he met the family who had protected him before but now the mother's husband was dead and they had only two cows. They were travelling south on their way to Takeo. He went with them to live with the Cambodian soldiers who supported the Vietnamese. He stayed with them a few days as he and the beautiful daughter liked each other very much. 'I knew the mother wouldn't want me for the daughter, I had no money', he said but the first few days were 'almost like old days.' Then the girl met a soldier with a wristwatch and lost all interest in Samreth. Although he understood, his feelings were hurt. His pride was strong and he knew he could never compete with a real wristwatch, so he left them and set off by himself. The mother, who had become fond of Samreth, gave him a piece of a golden ring to help him on his journey. He ran into a group of Khmer Serei soldiers (Free Khmer) and joined them briefly. They gave him a gun but there was so little ammunition he only fired it once or twice. Then one night he dreamed that his mother was alive and needed him. He had no doubts whatsoever that she was calling him and ran away the next day, leaving his gun behind. He cut pieces off the precious ring to buy food and even a bicycle ride towards the Thai border. He moved slowly but steadily.

Further along the road he was picked up by two Russian military advisers in a large black car driven by a Vietnamese who spoke both Cambodian and Russian. The Russians were drunk, boisterous and happy. They were dressed in white, in contrast to the black clothes of the Cambodian cadres or the dark grey of the Vietnamese. Imprinted on Samreth's memory is the first armoured tank that he saw. The top opened and a fair-haired giant with blue eyes climbed out: he was too stunned to be frightened. The Russians kept asking Samreth, through the interpreter, which he preferred – the Soviet Union or America. The driver taught Samreth to say in Russian, 'I love the Soviet Union and do not like America' – his ticket for a ride almost to the border.

I met Poutherein for the first time in San Francisco in 1996 but we had corresponded and spoken on the telephone before this. She and Kilen are both happier in the English language than Samreth or Sary so chatter began at once. She was easy to like. She is without guile, straightforward and generous. Poutherein inherited her father's mercurial and unreflective character. She is wonderfully attractive, not with Kilen's delicate beauty, but slim, taut and explosive. Her large black eyes crackle with spirit. When she is excited, as she often is, her voice grows raucous. She was aware of this as she told her story and apologized but the decibel count grew even louder. The past has done nothing to limit her impulsiveness. Like the good American she has become, she is ready to move on when necessary and she no longer has any fear of impermanence. She seemed happy to tell her story.

Poutherein found Houssara in Battambang after the city fell to the Vietnamese. Poutherein is enterprising, fearless, tense and extremely intelligent. She and Houssara managed to scrounge some salt from houses in the city that had been abandoned: they found nothing else but were grateful for this precious commodity. Together (Houssara was eight and she about thirteen) they set themselves up in commerce. Their salt made quite a nice capital. After days of searching Sary found them at their work and announced her intention to try, with Kilen, to get to the border camp called 07. (Only later did they discover that 07 was a lawless enclave for smugglers and that they would be safe only with the UN at Khao-I-Dang). Poutherein's legs were still swollen (she had never recovered from her severe attack of jaundice) and they were unwilling to leave their thriving business until all the salt was bartered or sold. Poutherein and Houssara promised to rejoin Sary and Kilen within a few days. No one had the remotest idea of the hardships and dangers they might face getting to the camp: vague rumours had reached them about the brutality of Thai soldiers and the mountains to be crossed, but after more than four years of the Khmer Rouge nothing frightened them. Sary left Poutherein and Houssara some rice from her meager supply and the salt was bartered for dried fish and *caramelle* (sweets). They had always been taught not to lie. However, clever as she was, Poutherein soon realized that this was a peacetime rule and both she and Houssara made up some whoppers. Their imagination was as great as their need. Houssara limped while she wailed and clutched her side in pain and a cart stopped almost at once. They were given a ride and even a little rice soup. After the first time it was easy. They met a man who befriended these poor beaten orphans and gave them some 'real rice', rather than the watery soup that they had been living on for over four years. He had a great deal of rice, an amazing amount (they neither wondered nor cared where it came from) and he also knew how to get to the border and promised to take them. But he told them that the border was not open at the moment and they must wait. He had to go back to Siem Riep, his home near Angkor Wat, to get more supplies and told them to wait where they were for his return. They waited and waited, maybe ten days, maybe more but he didn't come back. Any kind of travel was still dangerous so they were not surprised, just disappointed. They decided to leave without him. A brave – or foolhardy – decision. They were unaware of the risks involved but at that stage would probably have taken their chances anyway. Poutherein wrote a letter to thank the man for everything he had done for them – the rice and the encouragement of getting to the border – she hadn't forgotten all her manners or her mother's teaching. She pinned the note on the wall, as they were in one of the Cambodian houses made of straw and palm leaf. They never learned what happened to him, so many people disappeared, dropped out of sight they gave it little thought but they were sorry. They had some food and a small piece of gold earned from their salt-trading and they felt grown-up and invulnerable.

Then one day Poutherein lost Houssara. She had been

taking a nap in their shelter and woke up to find him gone. She looked for him everywhere, she asked everyone she could find but no one had seen him, or would admit to having seen him. She called and called 'Baou, Baou' (little brother) but there was no answer. She went back to the shelter in tears, desperate at the thought of going on without Houssara. There she saw him, sitting in the corner eating rice. It was night by then and all she could see were the whites of his eyes and his teeth. She was incensed. To get the rice he had told an elderly woman he had no mother, no family at all. Poutherein was outraged, she was his sister, his big sister, and the lies were supposed to be hers. He had not even mentioned that he had a sister, which was the final indignity. Sheepishly he offered to share his rice. She grabbed him and tied him to the central pole in their hut. She began to beat him in a blind rage and to choke him. He submitted to the beatings but when she began to choke him he made such horrible noises that Poutherein herself was frightened. 'Never, never leave me again,' she pleaded, and started to weep in distress. He promised and she proudly says she never hit or strangled him again.

They were still miles and miles from the camp, that much they knew. They learned that the land on the way ahead was mountainous and very dangerous, and that close to the border there were threatening Thai soldiers everywhere. Then Houssara went out (with Poutherein's permission) and came back saying, 'I got the news there is another way around.' Poutherein does not remember the name of the place they were headed for, only that the way to it was wild and mountainous. Carefully hiding the tiny piece of gold that was their profit from the sale of salt, they set out. They went up hill, down hill. Houssara at one point had to carry Poutherein she was so weak. Houssara was only eight but years of Khmer Rouge labour had made him strong. There was a vague sort of trail to follow and they went slowly. Neither of them had shoes. They rested until Poutherein regained some strength and then went on. Houssara went ahead at first to lead the way and warn her about ditches, water and other hazards. Then they met 'a guy with a big knife'. As they were so slow he passed in front of them. They hailed him, 'Hey, big guy where are you going?' It was now that her 'politic family' training was an advantage – she began talking and obviously did it very well because the 'big guy' not only offered to lead them but put Houssara on his shoulder as they walked along. When they stopped their new friend cooked rice and gave them some, together with some meat. 'Even meat, meat for the first time in years, dried beef, it was so good, so good!' said Poutherein. They went on until they came to a house like an abandoned temple where there were other people. There was 'another guy' there, a Laotian who spoke Cambodian and Thai and who took people across the border, for a price. Poutherein thought he looked like a criminal and wanted to have nothing to do with him. He asked the children if they wanted to go with them as they were going to Thailand. Poutherein refused saying she wanted to go to her mother who was (she thought at the time) in 07 camp. Poutherein then spotted 'activity' outside the temple. A fairly large group of people had arrived and someone was collecting from them. She asked what was going on and was told these people, too, were going to Thailand and they have to pay 'like two or three ounces of gold'. Ounces in Asia, she insisted, were heavier than ounces in America. There were three or four men organizing the people. The man in charge looked less frightening and friendlier. He came over to the children and told them that they were going to pass 07 camp and when they passed 'we can drop you off.. So Poutherein said OK. They lined up with the others and off they set. There was a trail of sorts but it was heavily mined and totally unusable, so they had to walk through the jungle. Their bare feet bled. Poutherein began to scream in pain. Houssara was stoical but he, too, was covered with blood. The others had shoes or at least rags wound around their feet, the children had nothing. Poutherein cried but after the others told her to be quiet, she cried softly. Houssara endured. He was more like his mother and Kilen, thought Poutherein. Having inherited her father's character she was more inclined to anger, even hysteria; she never weighed the consequences the way her eight-year-old brother did.

Three days and three nights they walked through the jungle, stopping rarely for a brief rest, eating their rice as they walked. They walked in single file through the dense undergrowth which snagged and tore at their arms and legs. At certain points the bushes and trees were so thick that only the head of the person directly in front was visible. They walked close together, as close as possible, the terror of getting lost always present. Poutherein bled so profusely that she gave up, she could no longer stay on her feet. She stopped for a bit to rest and found herself alone. The worst had happened. The others had gone on without her and she was lost. She began to call out for help but at first her voice was so weak no one heard her. She called 'Uncle, uncle' and at last the man in charge heard her and came back. He told her that she would get killed if she stayed there, she must get on her feet and walk but all she could do was nod her head. She was too weak, too exhausted and in too much pain to struggle any more. He was not an unkind man and he wanted to save this poor bloody child. He tied a rope around her waist and dragged her along. She was half-conscious but she felt relieved, someone was taking care of her. She has no idea how long this lasted. Sometimes she managed to stagger along on her feet, sometimes she was dragged along on her back. She was so dazed she no longer felt any pain, just wonder at all the blood oozing out of her.

They finally came to a clearing, the rope was untied and she fell in a heap on the ground to learn that she had been taken all the way into Thailand. Just as they felt the excitement, relief and joy of delivery, gunshots were heard and people began to scream, 'Thai soldiers, Thai soldiers'. It was shortly before daybreak but still fairly dark, and Poutherein could not see Houssara anywhere. She was far more worried about Houssara's disappearance than about the presence of the Thais. The Thais approached and told the whole group to come out and surrender as they knew where they were. Many people began to cry, Poutherein could not understand why. She kept calling for Houssara. 'Baou, Baou, come out, please Baou, come out,' she prayed but there was no sign of him. To this day no one quite knows what happened to Houssara. He remembers that a Laotian man threw him into the undergrowth to hide him from the Thai soldiers. He remembers nothing else until he found himself in one of the small camps at the border. He was with a Laotian family of husband, wife and three small children. They tattooed a number and a sign on his chest (still slightly visible) and used him as a slave. The father was kind but the mother beat him with a big stick. He ran away and somehow made his way to the camp where he found Kilen. At that point remembering and forgetting were all the same to this battle-scarred eight-year-old.

Poutherein and her entire group were ordered into the back of a lorry driven by the Thai soldiers. Several of the adults began to weep and moan. They felt certain that the Thais were going to kill them or send them back. Poutherein had, until then, heard only vague rumours of the Thai soldiers' cruelty. Several people had tried to escape before and had been turned back; they, however, were the fortunate ones as they were at least still alive. There were stories of Thai soldiers who pushed Cambodian refugees from a high cliff into a minefield and of soldiers using the returning refugees as target practice. Poutherein thought that nothing could be worse than Pol Pot and she tried to console some of the others. The lorry in which they were riding stopped at a training camp. Sounds of soldiers drilling at the break of dawn did not sound menacing to Poutherein but the others kept up the wailing. They were unloaded and herded into an enclosure outside one of the main buildings in the camp. The sight of the Thai flag flying over the barracks had a soothing effect on Poutherein. Nothing, nothing could be worse than Pol Pot she kept repeating until the others told her, quite forcibly, to shut up. They remained in the enclosure without food or water from around five in the morning until around three in the afternoon. They were fed minutes before the arrival of the Red Cross. This was obviously planned so that the Red Cross representatives could see for themselves the generosity of the Thais. The food, Poutherein remembers, was wonderful – pork and bean sprouts. Forgetting her manners she pushed her way ahead of some of her elders in order to get to the precious stuff, gobbled it down and asked for more. She no longer cared what anyone thought of her she was so hungry and the food was so magnificent.

The Red Cross nurses cleaned and bandaged her feet and her other wounds. It looked as though they were finally to be cared for and were safe at last. This relief did not last long, as the whole group was put into the back of another lorry and taken to a huge, dank room dug out of the hillside. A low wall of bamboo kept the men on one side and women on the other. Many of the men were wearing leg irons, they were convicted criminals. Poutherein, to her horror, found herself in a Thai jail charged with illegal entry. She felt abandoned. Then the Red Cross came and gave her a spoon, a bowl and a mat for sleeping. She stayed there for two or three weeks until she was taken into the barracks for questioning. There was a Cambodian interpreter who helped her and told her what to say. She insisted that she (a thirteen-year-old child swathed in bandages) did not come to Thailand to spy or to overturn the government, she only came, she said because of the war in her own country. Tense as she was, she remembered being pleased at once again telling the truth. Then one day, she is not sure how many days later only that her wounds had begun to heal, she saw several vans lined up before the prison. Names were called out. The first two vans went to Khao-I-Dang, her name was called out for the third van. It went not to Khao-I-Dang but to the transition camp of Buriram in Thailand, a privilege. Buriram was known as 'the ready camp' and arrival there was almost a guarantee of resettlement. There were sponsors for the refugees in Buriram, sponsors from all over the world, Germany, Australia, France, Italy even China. The refugees shrieked, 'CHINA who would want to go to China?' It was simple, you were registered and then someone came along and picked the orphan he wanted. Everyone thought Poutherein was an orphan (her respite from telling the truth was brief). It was made clear to her by the inter-preter and the others that for orphans doors were opened, so she became that much sought-after commodity, an orphan. She still held out hopes of seeing her mother but soon began to believe, as she had been told again and again, the best way to find her family again was to get to a 'third country' her-self. Whether this was true or not she did not know, every-one was adamant on the subject. A 'third country' was paradise, surely only good could happen to her there. She was taken into an office to be questioned by an American immigration official, a 'big guy'. Are there no small Americans, she wondered? His head was buried in a series of files, one of which was hers. He spoke a bit of Cambodian but most of the questioning was done through an interpreter. 'You have an uncle in France,' he said, 'Why do you want to go to America?' Then her political training took over. 'My father studied in America and he told me that America was the best place to live.' All this she said through the interpreter. Then she stood up forcing him to look at her straight in the eye as she said in English, as her father had taught her, 'AMERICA is the land of OPPORTUNITY'. 'You,' said the official, 'are going to America.'

She was happy. For several days she ate, slept on her mat, sang to herself and dreamed of her bright future. One day as she lay on her mat day-dreaming she heard her name called out over the loudspeakers. She was given a number – Americans love numbers she thought – and told to get ready to leave. She rolled up her mat and reported for her new life.

Kilen and Sary's stories were inextricably linked and this is what I managed to piece together. With the arrival of the Vietnamese the Khmer Rouge camps were broken up, but the family was so scattered (and communications non-existent) that only Kilen, Sary and Puit, the nine-year-old daughter, were able to find each other at first.

Kilen walked along the only road away from the paddy asking if anyone had seen her mother. An old man told her that Sary had passed him a short while ago and that if she hurried she could catch her. Weak and tired as she was she began to run and soon she saw Sary and Puit ahead of her. She began to call her mother and Sary turned. All she could say was, 'You, you is it really you?' as an exhausted Kilen threw herself into her mother's arms.

They knew that Sarin, Sary's parents and Noi, the eight-year-old boy, were dead but they knew nothing about the others and, quite naturally, they expected the worst. In

Battambang they found Poutherein and Houssara. It was there that Puit, the nine-year-old girl died, apparently from tetanus and lack of proper medication. It happened suddenly and terribly. Her muscles tightened until she had a fixed, joyless smile on her face, then she could no longer breathe. Sary and Kilen were helpless, and within forty-eight hours she was dead. Before she died she asked Sary to remove the elastic from her skirt and give it to Houssara as his shorts were held up with only an old piece of rope. Sary was so distraught she couldn't bring herself to carry out the child's wish. She couldn't even bring herself to look at the child's body and gave it over to be cremated to avoid contamination. The precious elastic was burnt together with the poor, rigid, little body. Only the children cried, Sary was speechless and tearless. Then when food became scarce once again, Sary decided they must try to get to the camps at the Thai border. At first the Vietnamese soldiers had given them food but then their own supplies diminished and were not replaced. There were two choices, says Kilen, stay and starve or try to get to the border. They chose to risk the trip. Poutherein was still very weak and her legs were so swollen she could scarcely walk so they left Houssara with her, together with some of their precious rice. Kilen and Sary set off by themselves, promising to send for the other two when they arrived safely at the border. It was unseasonably hot and Kilen worried about her mother, still dazed after the cruel death of her nine-year-old daughter. Kilen begged rides on bicycles. 'Please sir, uncle,' she would say and when someone agreed, she would call for her mother who would ride as far as she could and then wait for Kilen. They were told the road to Thailand was straight ahead. There was no danger of getting lost. Mostly they walked. Sleeping on the ground was no problem but the meager supply of food they brought with them dwindled daily. They had no shoes and the road was rough, the weather incredibly hot. They wound rags around their swollen feet and somehow hobbled towards the border.

They walked for eight days until they reached the Thai frontier. When Sary finally unbandaged her feet all her toenails came off. They were weary beyond belief, but they felt safe when they saw the many other Cambodians camped there. Kilen says that her first sight of electricity seemed to be a miracle: they had been living in the dark for so many years. She found it hard to believe the extent of her joy at seeing it. When you have nothing, she thought, then you appreciate electricity, even if it is not yours. Then she saw that there was food, bread and ice: people drinking soda pop from bottles. It was almost like her memories of before the war! There were many others camped there but, unlike themselves, they had food and supplies. Kilen and Sary had almost nothing. Terror and deprivation had made others hard, selfish and tight-fisted, says Kilen. No one offered them any food. Their only possession was a teapot, their only food, one can of rice. (The unit of measurement was a can of condensed milk which contained about 250 grams of rice.) Sary was too proud to beg, and although Kilen wasn't, she had little success. Sary went to look for wild leaves to cook with their rice and Kilen wandered around this wonderful, terrible place. She saw people drinking what looked like milk. It turned out to be filthy water. How can they drink that she wondered. It looked so awful, it gave her an idea. She took her precious teapot and found ten empty bottles which she tied, with vines, on to a bamboo pole. These she balanced on her shoulders and set out to find a source of clear water. The teapot was light and the bottles heavy so the pole was difficult to balance and as she walked she clinked and clanked. It was so dry she could not find any water. She came upon some people going the other way who had water, and she asked, 'Uncle, aunt, please tell me where you got the water'. They refused to tell her. They even made fun of her and called her stupid for asking. She looked at the sky and asked why she had been brought this far to starve among these mean people. Why wasn't I killed in Cambodia, she thought, why do I have to go through this? She walked along singing to keep her spirits up but when she found herself singing a Khmer Rouge work song she burst into tears. Suddenly she felt a splash on her face. She had stepped into a running stream. The water was clear blue with the blueness of purity, 'so clear, so clear' she said. She danced in the stream, doused herself in the glorious liquid, laughing and singing at the same time. Then she collected all the water that her bottles and teapot could hold and made her way back to the camp, slowly as her load was heavy. Once in the camp she sat by the road and called out, 'Please, sir, uncle, please, aunt, come buy my pure water, the finest water you have ever had.' She sold her entire stock and earned 15 baht (about 75 cents/45 pence). Never had she felt so proud as when she presented her earnings to Sary. Sary's excitement when she saw the blessed money was another reward, that and the bread and canned fish they bought for their supper.

It was so good, that first meal in their new lives. Kilen went everyday to her stream after this. Sometimes she could not sell the water, when it rained people weren't thirsty. A born entrepreneur, she cast about for a more permanent situation. She found a woman who made and sold rice noodles and asked if she could sit next to her as people were sure to be thirsty after eating. The woman had no time to bring water from the stream and welcomed Kilen: they established a partnership. She exchanged water for noodles: it worked beautifully. After her enterprise had made her almost 500 baht (25 U.S. dollars) she decided to branch out. As she said, 'I do more adventure things.' First Sary paid a man to bring

Poutherein and Houssara from Cambodia. The rest of the money was Kilen's capital. She saw some men with great loads of rice which they sold in the camp. Learning that they had run the risk of entering Thailand proper she determined to join them. 'Sir, uncle, can I come with you?' she asked. She was told it was impossible as she was a woman and women, if caught by Thai soldiers, were raped and even killed. The men were merely robbed and beaten. Undeterred, Kilen wrapped a cloth around her head and posed as a boy (at four in the morning not much is visible). Her clothes were loose, her hair completely hidden, no one could really see her. So, without even asking permission, she got in line and followed the men into Thailand. She went to buy rice, bargained with the Thais, came back to the camp and sold her rice. At the border were those who had made their way there to bring rice back into Cambodia for sale. They were her best customers. If the border was closed the price went up and Kilen became a war profiteer. She got up at four in the morning to cross the border where she bought rice and canned fish which Sary sold and by eight the same morning she was back selling her water. This was the everyday routine until representatives of the Red Cross came to where they were camped and promised to take them to Khao-I-Dang. Two days later a large lorry came to collect them and several others. Some of the people were reluctant to get into the lorry as it was driven by an armed Thai soldier with an even more heavily armed soldier seated next to him. Kilen and Sary were also wary but they scrambled into the back, Sary with her back to the side of the lorry, Kilen seated between her knees. They had been camped by the side of a deeply rutted mud track. The lorry was old, the motor noisy and the load heavy but it managed to chug along. After what seemed like hours they came to a crossroads. The road to the right was another crude track and led to mountains, the road

142

to the left was newly asphalted. When they stopped, one of the soldiers got out and went into the woods. The Cambodians crammed in the back were too frightened to do more than stand up to look out and try to discover where they were being taken. The back of the lorry began to smell of their fear. They had all heard of the dreaded mountain where the Thais had thrown thousands of refugees to their death. There was an unnatural silence as the motor started up again. When the driver turned to the left, there was a collective sigh of relief and Kilen found herself in tears. They soon stopped at Khao-I-Dang and when they saw their first sign of foreign faces they felt that they had at last been rescued. It was here that Sary recognized a picture of Samreth, and they were eventually reunited.

Safe in the hands of the United Nations relief workers, Sary began to dream again: she had not dreamed in years. She dreamed of Sarin, she dreamed of her 'tall brothers' and her dead children. One night she dreamed of Sihanouk. He told her that he would grant her every wish but first Kilen must dance for him. Sary believed this to be a sign and persuaded Kilen to dance again. Sary was criticized by other camp members for keeping Kilen away from English lessons and letting her dance instead. 'The dancing is important, too,' she said, little knowing how true this was to be. Kilen's dancing was to prove a turning point in all our lives.

There were several young girls who danced at Khao-I-Dang. The dancing was the camp's main entertainment. A raised platform served as a stage. Sometimes the girls were sent to outlying camps to perform. On one of her last performances before leaving for Italy – at a small camp near Khao-I-Dang – a larger than usual crowd had gathered and a group of ragged little boys had pushed their way to the front. After the performance the very dirtiest and most bedraggled tugged at Kilen's skirt and said, 'I think you might be my sister'. Kilen recognized Houssara at once, threw her arms around him, running sores, snotty nose and all. When she came back to Khao-I-Dang she screamed for her mother and Samreth. Samreth came running at once but Sary was unable to move, so conditioned by loss and misery she could not bring herself to believe Kilen that Houssara was really there. Kilen and Samreth went to the camp's director, the admirable Tom Generico, and he arranged for Houssara's transfer to Khao-I-Dang the next day. The children were ecstatic but when he arrived Sary could only stare at him in wonder. It was some time before she could bring herself to touch him.

Through Kilen's dancing they also made contact with Poutherein. While dancing in another camp Kilen was recognized as Sarin's daughter by the widow of a former minister who was on her way to the U.S. She promised to look out for Poutherein and indeed met her in Buriram, the transitional camp where people were processed for immigration to the United States. They could make no direct contact with her but at least they knew she had survived.

PART V

They are thriving I see. I hope they always thrive
Whether in Italy, England or France.
Let them dream as they wish to dream. Let them dream

Of Jesus, America, maths, Lego, music and dance.

WHEN OUR FIRST anniversary came around – 19 February, 1982 – we decided to celebrate. Sary was so much stronger and the children well established in school. It was a full year of achievement. We felt we were all owed a party. There was a newly opened Chinese restaurant in Florence, a real novelty at the time. Simon was at Westminster School in London, but the rest of us, dressed in our best, drove into Florence. There were ten of us in all: three Vietnamese, four Cambodians, Lisa, John and myself. Trinh and Tuyen took over the ordering and the Chinese flowed to everyone's amusement. We thought the food delicious although the Orientals had considerable reservations. There was a great deal of laughter, John amazed everyone by touching his nose with his tongue, Tuyen wiggled his ears, Samreth had a beer that went right to his head. We giggled about nothing in particular as though it was a first-time happiness for us all.

Suddenly I saw Tuyen reach across the table to Sary and slap her face. I realized she had had a seizure, her head was shaking uncontrollably and she was unconscious for what seemed an eternity. Samreth began to sob, Kilen turned pale and led Houssara into another room. Lisa called an ambulance and she and I took Sary to the nearest hospital. By the time we arrived at the hospital Sary had regained consciousness and although weak was coherent. The examination found nothing wrong with her so we brought her home shortly before midnight. John had stayed to pay the bill and he and Tuyen drove the children home.

It was as though the euphoria was too much for Sary. She had kept steady for all the years of horror and now at last, when she saw her children safe, an invisible hand had lifted a latch and all the blackness inside of her was released. When Lisa and I got Sary home Samreth stopped sobbing and Kilen made tea for everyone. We did not disturb Houssara who had curled up on the floor and purred himself to sleep. Tuyen picked him up and valiantly carried him the four floors up to his room without waking him. Children tend to have little or no knowledge of life other than their own, nature's protection against the outside world which can so often be baffling, precarious and frightening. When I thought of what these children had seen and known, I would shudder. For most children evil is just a rumour from some strange elsewhere, at most a film or a story. To these children it had a name and a face. There was nothing of the glamour and excitement of imaginary evil for them, just the gloom, the desolation, the slavery of the real thing. I would look at these children, so familiar and so dear, and wonder, try to imagine their other life. Somewhere inside were ghosts of horror, hunger, bloodshed, terror and with all my love I could never reach them. I could listen, I could weep for them, but the burden was theirs. One night we were watching a film on television: the Errol Flynn version of *Kim*. In one of the scenes Kim places a burr next to the skin of an infant to make him cry so that his 'Holy Man' can cure him, and be rewarded by the infant's mother. Houssara, who was nine at the time, groaned. He was visibly upset by the scene. 'He only did it because he was hungry, so it's not really bad,' he said. He was relieved when both Samreth and John agreed (in Cambodian and Italian). He had a highly developed moral sense, especially for a child his age, although, like most children, he could see little or no difference between a great wrong and a small one. Samreth had worried that

Houssara would eventually suffer guilt because of his confession to a Khmer Rouge cadre that his father had been a
senator.

Samreth was inclined to talk about his experiences with
the Khmer Rouge as an adventure. He had us laughing as he
showed how he and two friends managed to get an extra
ration of the dreadful and sparse food they were given. He
treated us to an elaborate performance, placing a series of
chairs in a line that led up to the cooking pot – guarded this
time by a benevolent Houssara. Then he danced in and out
of the line of chairs, a mad, manic, magical version of musical chairs. When least expected he was at the front of the line
time and time again. He wept easily, noisily and copiously
but never about events in Cambodia – those he spoke of with
laughter or rage. He wept excessively when John left home
to go on a business trip. He wept when he left for Oxford to
stay with James, and wept even more violently when he left
Oxford for home. Any parting completely unnerved him. He
couldn't bear an unhappy ending in a film or on television
and would leave halfway through if he had any suspicions
about the final reel. Samreth, who joked about his blood-
spattered companions in Cambodia, was appalled at any
filmed violence. He would press his hands tightly over his
ears and bend his head down as far as possible to escape.
Kilen was the same, but about sex. The first film I took the
children to see was John Boorman's version of *Excalibur*. I
thought a myth about King Arthur and chivalry would be
just the thing. Houssara and I were the only ones who actually saw the film: Samreth and Kilen had their heads down
most of the time.

The older two were more, not less, afraid than most children of their age, and not at all shy or embarrassed at
expressing their fear. At first I put that down to the strangeness of their new world. Certainly in Cambodia each had

shown bravery and daring, far exceeding most children's experience and under the most forbidding circumstances. Then, little by little, I came to believe that, unlike more fortunate, protected children, they had learned to trace the consequences of danger to the bitter end. A search for wild oranges could lead to rape and a bloody head. A hand stretched out to help a friend could be shattered by the blow of a rifle butt. They were on the lookout for any portent, any premonitory sign, mystical or imagined or real. Many childhood terrors seem to centre around people: the wicked stepmother, the cruel older sister, the sinister man in black, the bogeyman. To the children the terror was always personified by the figure of 'Pol Pot'. I once asked Kilen what Pol Pot looked like. I had seen only a blurry photograph of him in a newspaper. She had never even seen a picture of him yet she told me she knew his face from dreams and that it never changed. Once she started to draw me a picture of the face in her dreams. She got no further than the cap and the outline of the head when her hands began to tremble so severely that she had to stop.

Change was difficult for them all – even for Houssara who was only eight. Simple things such as using a knife and fork, sleeping between sheets, working to a time schedule, were new to them, and like most new things, bewildering. Houssara still talks about the strangeness of his first night here: the mattress with its magical springs and the fact that he was put to bed with electric lights on the stairway to his room. Unheard of, new and prodigious marvels that he was determined to understand. In the early days I often found him standing as close as possible to the refrigerator, a hand, palm up, against its side, trying, I learned later, to figure out why the cold stayed inside and not out. He was determined to understand how things worked, to learn. He made me realize that for some children intellectual curiosity can be a desire as strong as other more basic drives.

Houssara was the only one who did not suffer in the winter; in fact it was difficult to make him dress warmly enough. He also had a very high tolerance for pain. Falls from bicycles and later motor-bikes distressed him for the damage to the bike, not for the bloody head or dislocated shoulder suffered. He once fell from his bicycle into a field of stinging nettles. Because it was summer he was bare to the waist and was immediately covered with ugly red blisters. I came upon him, in his room, with his face turned to the wall, biting a cloth to keep from crying: he was nine. A psychotherapist who worked with victims of Nazi persecution and their children came to the house as a lunch guest, not in his professional capacity. Naturally he was fascinated by the children. His professional opinion differed from ours. He told us that adjustment would be far more difficult for Houssara than the others since he had no cultural memories to fall back on. The two older children had been to school, spoke and wrote their own language, and had felt part of a nation and its heritage. It is true that Houssara was illiterate in any language until he was nine and never really had a 'first language'. His spoken Cambodian is a family joke (he has never learned to write it). Although he had more trouble forming his letters and never acquired the dexterity of the other two, his social adjustment came much more easily than theirs. Actually, the expert's reasoning did not hold as none of the children had really known Cambodia, they had all been born into war and the Khmer Rouge. They were never homesick. The city of their birth had been abolished. Even Sary dreamed of another world, a life so much a part of the past that she could not communicate it to the children.

Samreth was so full of charm and so romantically beautiful that he had girls beating a path to our front door from the time he was fourteen. Strangely, even this success did not give him confidence. Old superstitions had such a hold on him that he continued to put more faith in amulets and fortune-tellers than in his own talents. He believed that music and art were not serious subjects for a man and that his natural gifts were unimportant. A friend of ours in Florence, Harold Acton, was particularly kind to the children, giving them all lovely presents. He was interested in all things Oriental so Samreth gave him in return a tiny statue of Buddha that he had always worn on a string around his neck. It was a crudely made little figure of no intrinsic value, but Harold was touched. The day after the present giving Samreth took to his bed convinced he was going to die. Doubled up in pain, writhing violently on his bed moaning, his skin the soft grey-green Southeast Asians get instead of pallor, he terrified me. Kilen rescued us both: Samreth from the doctor that I was ready to call, me from the fright I felt. He knew with absolute certainty, Kilen told me, that Buddha and his own good fortune had deserted him since he had given the little figure away. I bit my tongue from saying 'nonsense!' Kilen explained, carefully, softly and painstakingly to Samreth that his Buddha was now in the hands of an old man, a good and kind old man, and that Buddha himself would be pleased as the elderly are more in need of good fortune than the young. Samreth gave one final howl, rushed into the bathroom where he stayed for several minutes and came out, cured. To this day I do not know, nor would I ever ask, how much Kilen believed what she said. What I did believe was that having faced a 'reality' so malevolent and savage, Samreth needed to believe in magical powers that ruled both matter and nature. These beliefs took a long time to disappear, if they ever did completely. He told me of bands worn around soldiers' heads that kept them safe from bullets, of magical hair that kept growing within a tiny vial. I could only listen without comment, and hope my face didn't betray me. He believed with such necessity and force.

Yet it was Samreth who could see clearly the difference between what he considered 'rational' magic and fantasy. Bo and his cousins, Peng and Ang, were convinced that there were 'Germans' hiding in the deep end of the swimming pool (too much television obviously). John and I had failed to prove to them it wasn't so. Only Samreth by an elaborate series of dives and stories allayed their fears. 'You must,' he told them, 'believe only in good spirits in this country.' He was the Pied Piper, children and animals and girls followed him everywhere. (John bought him a recorder which he played by ear and which added to the effect.)

Samreth was on the lookout for *offese*, a wonderful Italian word that has more to do with loss of dignity than an actual insult. I have had experience with Oriental male pride, a universal trait, but never have I seen it stronger than in Samreth. I once jokingly called him 'Signor Samreth' and he was offended: he thought I was making fun of his lack of position. One afternoon in early summer we were all outside delighting in the sun's warmth. Kilen and I were collecting wildflowers; Samreth was high up in the holm oak; Houssara was dashing about on his new bicycle and Trinh was making flower chains in a vain attempt to attract Bo's attention. Bo's only real interest was in Houssara and his bicycle. Wanting to be helpful, Sary picked up a scythe and began attacking some stray weeds. Samreth came down from the tree with a face as grim as stone and grabbed the scythe from her hands. His mother, his father's wife, would never again do peasant's work.

Samreth had many talents: one summer he discovered the piano. We have an upright Japanese model, bought for our son Simon when he was nine years old. It was usually out of tune but for Samreth it was ideal: compact and available. James started him out on a Bach Prelude. Samreth had never touched a piano, had scarcely seen one before, but was musically sensitive and played with manifest enjoyment. We held a family conference with James and decided that he should have proper lessons. Interestingly, he loved Bach and Mozart and simple Bartók but was hopeless with any of the romantics and when he tried Gershwin it was a disaster. We took him to hear Richter play, it was his first concert and he adored it. When Richter concluded a Sonata with a great bravura flourish, Samreth burst out laughing, a proper reaction and one I felt certain Richter would have approved.

All four came to Italy provided with chest X-rays to prove there was no TB and a medical certificate (a printed form with half the spaces blank) that indicated, at best, a cursory examination. They also brought their traditional medication. Their equivalent of Trinh's 'dragon's tooth' was a solid round object, coin-shaped and about two inches in diameter. When any child had a headache, stomach trouble or just general malaise he went to Sary who dipped the coin in oil and scraped lines on arms, legs and back until she raised ugly red welts all over the sufferer's body. Without fail the patient declared himself cured. Sary, however, recognized the limits of her cure when Samreth came down with a severe case of shingles. She was terrified, thinking she could see traces of her nine-year-old daughter's symptoms. The cruelty of losing her first born was a thought too horrible to bear. Samreth was never in any real danger although in acute pain, speechless and numb with fear. Our GP was heroic and not only came to see Samreth twice a day for the first few days but spent time calming Sary's fears as well. After a week or so Samreth declared himself well, and the doctor agreed. The coin cure was never used again.

*

The children made lasting and in some cases passionate, friendships. That, to me, says something for Italian sensibility as well as the children's charm. Like most people confronted by completely different surroundings they were inclined to see only virtues or defects, never a mixture. Kilen thought the girls in her class were all lovely, even the plainest. She loved the way they walked, so different from the flat-footed tread of Cambodian women. What a wonderful and elegant thing a Western instep was. She loved my footprints when I came out of the swimming pool and would place her tiny, completely flat prints next to my enormous ones. She deplored the lack of respect, as she saw it, to old people. One day she came home indignant at having seen an elderly woman cross the street unaided. She admired the freedom of girls her age although she never took advantage of it. She was still terrified of men, not boys her own age, just men. Her shyness was no affectation, her timidity about her body no mere prudishness. When I first bought her a bathing suit she giggled and refused to wear it. Finally, during a very hot summer she came up to the pool but only when there were no males present.

Her fear of men was in a large measure justified and not only by her Cambodian experiences. At Khao-I-Dang she slept under Sary's bed as the Thai soldiers often came into the shelters at night with flashlights on the lookout for pretty refugee girls. She found it difficult to believe she was safe. Once when we were rebuilding a fallen wall near the house, one of the workers, a handsome blue-eyed Sicilian, asked her if she would like to go to the movies with him. She was terrified, shaking her head and staring at the ground. With me she became hysterical, gulping and weeping and saying, 'If my father were alive he wouldn't insult me so.' I felt rather sorry for the good-looking lad. For all the rest of the time he worked at the house he brought her little presents: flowers, chocolates and once a piece of Sicilian pottery which we still have. Fortunately, the wall was soon finished.

Kilen willed herself to be brave during the day but at night the terror took over and many is the time I have gone to her when she screamed and found her face wet with tears. Little by little the fear subsided and she became preoccupied by the kind of worries I could understand. When she first turned to me in acute distress because 'No one understands me', I wanted to kiss her. It was the same story that I had heard from my own children during their teens and I could somehow cope. Poor Kilen, being a teenager is difficult enough under any circumstances. She was a complicated mixture of innocence and experience – mixture that could easily have destroyed older and wiser heads than hers. As time passed her self-confidence increased and with it came a gentle, but determined, calm.

Kilen was a dancer and she performed the Classical Royal Cambodian dances. Sary had begun to limber up Kilen's hands when she was little as required by that exotic art. One of our first purchases in Italy for them was a piece of silver-threaded cloth so that her mother could make her a new costume. The dancing was a delight to us and to our friends. One cynical, and slightly drunken, journalist burst into tears at her performance. Several of Simon's friends were secretly in love with her but were too much in awe to tell anyone but John or myself. Her appalling history and her fragile beauty intimidated healthy, pampered teenagers. Once I told her that one of Simon's friends, a tall, incredibly handsome blond youth was in love with her – I couldn't resist. She answered, 'Oh, no, he is sky and I am earth. It could never be.'

Kilen's shyness disappeared when she danced, but the minute the dance was over she ran from the room. I was fascinated by the way she used her fingers. They could do wonderful things, those fingers, they could see in the dark, explore the world, anything. The dancing itself was exquisite and strangely non-sexual. I once asked her if she danced in her mind as well as her body and she said, 'Of course'. She sang softly as she danced. The words sounded hypnotically similar, the sounds coming from deep in her throat, almost from the nape of her neck in the Oriental manner.

When the Khmer Rouge forced her to work in the rice paddy the dance training helped her. She showed me the rhythmic motions, the bending and graceful hand movements that looked so tender and were in actual fact back-breaking. She sang the songs devised by the Khmer Rouge to lighten her work, or more properly, to speed it up. The songs were unusually musical, not like most work songs that depend entirely on rhythm. She moved her tiny golden hands delicately as she planted the imaginary green shoots, stepping back after each planting so that the entire process became one perfect movement, like water flowing. I found it difficult to believe that anything so aesthetically lovely could be, in reality, a murderous form of labour.

Sary grew stronger during that first year and her depressions weaker and further apart. She had never, even during her extreme lows, lost her dignity. Suffering may indeed ennoble, but the old adage holds true only if there was something worthy to begin with. She was a wonderful cook and often prepared some delicious Cambodian dishes. I was sorry when she gave up wearing sarongs and chose Western dress. She looked so lovely in the draped sarong and seemed to enjoy teaching me how it worked. Practicality took over though and the sarongs were replaced by skirts and later even by trousers. As the months passed the lines around her eyes faded and the sadness in them almost disappeared. Then one could imagine her as the eighteen-year-old bride dressed in her finest, gold-threaded sarong, hair loose and garlanded with flowers as she walked under a canopy through the streets of Phnom Penh.

Through the Red Cross we had learned that her daughter, Poutherein, barely one year older than Kilen, was alive and well and married in San Francisco. She was considered the family intellectual because from her early childhood she had been interested in politics and she was called 'the baby politician'. She was also considered the family beauty because she was slightly taller and much fairer than the others. I have always found this tyranny of skin colour and the widely accepted preference for paleness strange but it certainly exists. Houssara, who is by far the darkest of the family, has always come into his share of teasing. It has, however, remained just that, good-natured teasing without offense received or given. The practice has surprised many of our friends who are accustomed to Western attitudes about colour.

After Poutherein had been separated from Houssara she made the rest of the journey alone. At this point Poutherein had no idea how many, if any, of the family had survived. In the camp she met and married a Cambodian-Chinese, twice her age, whose name was on a list to go to America: she was fifteen. It may have begun as a marriage of convenience but within a short time it turned into a love match. Her first child was born before her seventeenth birthday. Puit, her nine-year-old daughter, had come to Sary in a dream. 'I could feel her soft baby hand', she said. In the dream she told her mother that she was well and in her sister's womb. The birth of Poutherein's daughter, Mary, shortly after, gave Sary great comfort.

Sary had two sisters whose whereabouts were not known until later. We got a suspect letter written in barely decipherable English, postmarked Singapore, from a sailor who claimed to be in touch with them. He could help them, he wrote, if we sent him some dollars or two Swiss watches. How he ever found our address we never learned. All attempts to trace him or them were fruitless. After that first letter we never heard from him again. We finally made contact with the sisters who were still in Phnom Penh. In November of 1991 two great friends of ours, the noted art historians, John Fleming and Hugh Honour, went to Cambodia. It was shortly after the Civil War ended, the peace treaty was signed and UN-sponsored elections were in sight. I asked them if they would mind taking some money to one of Sary's sisters begging them not to put themselves at risk. They went with their driver/interpreter to the address I had been given, a fairly large office building, and sent the interpreter inside to find her. They went at the close of the working day so as not to disturb her too much. The interpreter had no trouble at all and she came out to their car at once. 'What did she look like?' I wanted to know. 'Like an office worker', said John. She took the money and letter I had written, smiled, thanked them and put everything into the basket of her bicycle without any hesitation, fear or fuss, as though it was an expected everyday occurrence, and rode away. Later she even came to their hotel and brought a brief letter and piece of Cambodian cloth as a present for Houssara. 'Couldn't have happened six months ago', said the interpreter. Sary is now in touch with both sisters regularly.

The Cambodians got several letters from friends and relatives who somehow managed to find us. One, for Samreth, was postmarked Moscow where a school-friend was studying engineering. He had fled to Laos and, as a bright student, was sent from there to study in the Soviet Union. Another, for Sary, arrived from the daughter of Son Ngoc Than who was living incognito in Vietnam where her father had died in prison. The letters were always answered but we never heard further. We tried sending money to Sary's friend in Vietnam but this was before the 'thaw': it arrived after a delay of months and such a healthy chunk was taken by the government that there was little left for Sary's friend. All this we learned much later when the friend made her way to Canada and got in touch with Sary through the amazing system of refugee information. Mysteries remain. The mother of a Cambodian friend of ours who had long been thought dead turned up in Washington, D.C., unexpectedly and joyfully. I learned long ago not to question too closely, just to be pleased at any good news.

There was also Sary's youngest brother, Vancy, who lived in Paris. Vancy had been at the Sorbonne when the Khmer Rouge took over and unlike most of his fellow students, refused to go back to Cambodia when Pol Pot urged their return. He had a moment of doubt when he went to the airport to say goodbye to nine of his friends. The enthusiasm with which they left to help re-build their country was almost, but happily not completely, contagious. All nine, including Vancy's first cousin, ended up in the notorious Tuol Sleng prison and were murdered together with other returning 'intellectuals'. Vancy had married a French girl and when Sary first came to Italy we made contact with them and they promised to come to visit with their young daughter. Sary was the eldest of seven, after her were the three 'tall brothers', the two missing sisters, then came the baby, Vancy. His wife, Silvie, was the daughter of a successful doctor and the family spent a month each summer at the parents' villa in the south of France. They drove to Florence from there and arrived late one Friday afternoon, Silvie driving a conservative family car loaded with equipment for two-year-old Jade and presents for everyone. Sary had talked so much about her 'tall' brothers' beauty I wasn't prepared for Vancy. Slightly under six feet, he was incredibly handsome sporting a modified Afro hair style that was then the height of fashion, dressed tastefully in forest green. We learned later that as a student in Paris he supplemented his income working as a photographer's model. Silvie was almost as tall and handsome in a raw-boned way that made me think of Joan of Arc. Jade was a paler edition of her father.

An initial shyness was inevitable: John and I had anticipated it and did our best to keep things moving. Silvie, like Sary, was undemonstrative and Vancy too overwhelmed to do more than hug them all again and again: the real excitement was left to the children who rushed about smoothing cushions to entice the visitors to sit, bringing unwanted drinks and generally screaming their heads off. Late that first night I awoke and noticed lights still on in the *salotto*. Thinking someone had forgotten to turn them off I went upstairs to find Sary seated very close to Vancy, holding his hand as she spoke softly to him. Tears were streaming down his face as she told her story. It was past three in the morning.

Sary went to visit in Paris and returned with an impressive array of cheeses for John. Silvie had gone to a great deal of trouble and there were precise instructions on their proper care and consumption as well as two bottles of wine to be drunk only with two specific cheeses. John and I gorged happily as the Cambodians found the whole thing smelly and disgusting. It was also decided that Kilen and Sary would spend a few weeks with Vancy and Silvie at the sea the following summer. We made rather complicated plans for that summer (their second in Europe). Sary had somehow made contact with a cousin who lived in Paris. I was to drive all four to England with a stopover in Paris to see the cousin whose son had, alas, been one of the nine who returned to Cambodia. I would then leave Samreth and Houssara with

James in Oxford and take the others to the south of France.

Driving through France (back roads, not Autoroute) has always delighted me and this trip was better than ever. It was a treat to see familiar and admired sights through the eyes of sensitive, receptive passengers to whom everything was new and primarily wonderful. The first night we stayed at an inn between Pont Arlier and Ornans as I wanted to show them the Courbet Museum the next morning. There are a few minor works in the museum but its attraction to me is the setting; the clear, pure sound of running water from the wild river nearby, the unspoilt village and the pleasure the town takes in Courbet, its illustrious son. No hushed reverence, no ostentation, only the feeling that this particular boy did well. We wandered into the village with Samreth pointing out a statue of a fisherboy in the main square: it was charming, and a small model statue in his studio suggests that it was inspired, if not executed, by Courbet himself.

Then on to Paris, a part of Paris I nor any of my Parisian friends had ever seen before. Boulogne Brillancourt is a stop on the *périphérique* south of Paris and we found the exit without too much difficulty. Finding the cousin's house, a rather battered building of the turn of the century built around a centre courtyard, required more ingenuity. This particular part of the city seemed to be inhabited primarily by Orientals. The concierge herself was Laotian but her French was fluent and had even acquired the proper churlish tone. Kilen and I climbed the several flights of stairs to the cousin's flat leaving the boys below with a nervous and emotional Sary. There was no answer to our repeated knocking and calling but we were heard by a neighbour. A tiny, very old lady who looked like a benevolent witch told us, in heavily accented French, that the cousin was at work and would be home in an hour or so. All three of us spoke uneasy French as we explained ourselves to each other. 'I, too, am a refugee,' said this minute creature, 'I know what it is like.' She began to cry, with joy she assured us, as she would be able to see us happily reunited. She had escaped with her parents when the revolution swept Czar Nicholas from the throne and was finishing her days with her great-grand-daughter here in Boulogne Brillancourt.

The Cambodians are a bit vague about family relation-ships, husband and wife call each other brother and sister and full names are not always known. Villages were not organized the way they were in China and Vietnam and even in the cities few records were kept. Ancestor worship did not exist, only the nuclear family was important. So I am still not certain of the exact degree of relationship of the three family members we met; Sary's cousin, the cousin's cousin and his wife. That night we all ate at the local (delicious) Vietnamese restaurant. They were dignified, courageous, considerate and utterly charming. Kilen assured me that the tears each shed wouldn't last long and she was right. It was an exquis-ite banquet with each offering dishes and compliments to us all. An evening full of pale noise and nostalgic, bitter-sweet laughter.

We were lucky with the Channel Ferry. We found a place on the first one we tried and everyone was brave, silently so, during the adventure of parking in the echoing, crowded hold. We found a table in the top deck bar where Sary and Kilen sat rigidly during the entire voyage refusing drink, food or toilette. First Houssara and then Samreth explored the ship, each in his own way. Samreth struck up a conver-sation with two pretty girls who bought him sandwiches and drinks. Houssara climbed up and down the stairways noting with interest the different vibrations the motors made on each deck. Then he discovered the slot machine. I confess to a weakness for the damned machines myself and had been playing, unsuccessfully, when Houssara asked for a go. I gave him two of my last tenpenny pieces. He hit the jackpot on the first try. Business at the bar came to a standstill and the bartender came running out with a plastic sack to catch the money – £150 in tenpenny pieces makes quite a racket as it jumps out at one. Houssara was calm and dignified as he brought his sack to the table where Sary and Kilen sat, unlike Samreth and myself who made no effort to conceal our excitement.

We had four days in London. The 'whiteness' of the city disturbed Samreth; Kilen called the parks 'tame jungle'; Houssara was miffed that the Queen was not at home when I took them to see the changing of the guard. Then on to Oxford where all five of us crowded in on James. After three busy days, seeing friends, punting on the river and wandering about the university, we left the boys with James and took off for France. I knew that Samreth who spoke passable English would have no trouble but I worried, needlessly, about Houssara. He made friends with the talkative, enthusiastic mother of an English friend. He couldn't possibly understand what she was saying (even I had trouble) but her goodness was clear to him, or maybe it was her loneliness.

His great friend however was Danuta, the beautiful young Polish wife of Tim Garton Ash. Danuta knew no more English than Houssara and neither Italian nor Cambodian. He had neither of her languages, German nor Polish but their friendship was real and they seemed to understand everything the other said. 'She looks like Danuta' was for years Houssara's highest form of praise. Both boys had very definite ideas about female beauty. Only Kilen wasn't interested: she seemed almost to dislike or at least to be afraid of her own beauty.

At first only Samreth was curious about Florence so John took him to see the city. John was fascinated by Samreth's

164

uneducated but nearly unerring eye. The simple Renaissance lines and the coolness of the Pietra Serena appealed to him in the same way as Mozart and Bach were to do. Without any prompting from John he disliked the façades of the Duomo and Santa Croce. And when John took him to the Pazzi Chapel he sat down, crossed his legs and pressed his hands together in the attitude of Buddhist prayer. John went outside so he would not disturb Samreth and came back after a few minutes to find a radiant boy whirling around with outstretched arms.

When Samreth finished Middle School he wanted to follow his friends into the Liceo Scientifico which, as we feared, turned out to be a mistake. He did his best, but understood little of what was expected of him scholastically. He did well in English lessons and excelled in technical drawing. He failed everything else but here again he became the special 'pet', even of the teachers who despaired of him in class. It was through the drawing teacher that we got him accepted at the Scuola d'Arte di Porta Romana (the Art School at Porta Romana) where he really belonged, and where he went on to get his *Maturità*, the Italian equivalent of a Baccalaureate, so much more than a high-school diploma. His drawings were delicate, intimate and extremely skilful. I have in my bedroom one of his first efforts, a copy of a De la Tour portrait from the Louvre which, although accurate, looks surprisingly like a lovely Oriental girl.

Kilen's obsession with food continued. She became plump, too plump for her tiny frame. She seemed destined to put on weight until she burst, until one night watching television in our bedroom where we all piled on our huge bed, she saw a classical ballet and was enchanted. She started to diet and began dancing lessons the next week. Classical ballet did not work with the flat heel and toe movements of Cambodian dancing but she kept at it with dogged enthusiasm. A Western instep was indeed a great and wonderful thing she told me but the other girls used their fingers foolishly.

Houssara meanwhile was enthralled constructing buildings and machines with his newly acquired Lego. I regret that I did not keep at least one or two of his most imaginative inventions. To Sary he became her engineer brother although she had to bend a Buddhist rule or two to make the dates match.

'Not yet, not yet . . .' I kept saying to myself by the third summer. It was clear that some changes would come, must come, should come but exactly what I wasn't sure, and, frankly, I was in no hurry. About the others I couldn't be sure. Sary was so much stronger in every way and Samreth felt himself a man. They would soon, if they hadn't already, feel it necessary to make their own decisions, to feel that they could no longer pledge their futures to us. It was natural for them to wish for a life that no longer depended on our powers but on their own. Would our family bond dissolve, our union end, when there was no longer any need for it, I wondered? Today I know my worries were needless. A genuine love on both sides and common goals still pull us together although 'distance and duties' do indeed divide us.

That summer Kilen went to the south of France alone to stay with her uncle Vancy and his family. We sent Samreth to the sea as a paying guest with an Italian family to improve his Italian, took Houssara with us to Istria and sent Sary to San Francisco to see her other daughter, Poutherein, and to meet her granddaughter. Since the older children were still away, Houssara and I were to drive to the airport in Rome to meet Sary on her return, and bring her back to Florence. Monday evening we were all, together with our friend Elizabeth, in our bedroom watching a re-run of *Roman*

Holiday on television. John was explaining to Houssara about the scene of *La Bocca della Verita* when the phone rang. It was Sary in her halting Italian. I told her that Houssara and I would be waiting for her when she stepped off the plane. She hesitated and then put Poutherein on the line. 'My mom,' said an Americanized Poutherein, 'was married today and won't come back.' 'Married!' I shrieked as Houssara turned grey. 'His face, dear God,' said Elizabeth, 'the look on his face!' None of us could find anything to say, we were all struck dumb by the astonishing and unexpected announcement. John, as usual, came to the rescue. He went downstairs and opened a bottle of champagne we happened to have in the refrigerator and we all drank to Sary's health, even Houssara. The champagne improved our spirits and sent Houssara to sleep, as intended.

Poutherein had arranged everything: Sary had married a green card. It was up to us to tell the others. Two days later Houssara and I drove the six hours to the sea to tell Samreth in person. In the throes of first love and sexual experience Samreth seemed to take it well and some of his coolness rubbed off on Houssara. Kilen was due back from France within a few days so we decided to wait until then to tell her. She was appalled. Fortunately school started soon after her return and she began her last year at Middle School with her usual consuming interest. A few weeks later I came home to find Samreth, tears streaming down his face, on the phone with his mother. She had just told him that she was arranging for the younger two to come to America but that she preferred that he stay in Italy.

What followed was not easy for anyone. A struggle began between Sary and ourselves for the children. I think you could say we all gained a bit and lost a bit. We were respectful of one another and the true affection was as strong as ever but the struggle was real. She, naturally, wanted the children to join her in California. We made a sort of compromise: I began working on the papers that would allow Kilen to emigrate to California. Her mother wanted, and needed her the most.

The fourteen months that elapsed between Sary's marriage and Kilen's departure were difficult for us all, but also personally rewarding for me as Kilen and I became very close. Truthfully, I never worried too much about Kilen in America, knowing her strength of character. What I perceived as the dangers of America wouldn't apply to her. I did worry, desperately, about the boys, especially Houssara. Chameleon that he was (by necessity in the past), to be thrown into an alien and perhaps violent atmosphere without adequate protection seemed to me a prescription for disaster. For a twelve-year-old with his history, without a language of his own, to start all over in school, abandoning what he had learned with such difficulty and leaving his devoted friends was too much to ask of him. True, he would be within a loving family, but a family that was itself struggling to get to grips with yet another world. Samreth's talents were obvious, Houssara's less so. He was good at mathematics though not instinctively brilliant the way Samreth was. He was a builder, a fixer, a theorizer: he was searching for his own special path which led eventually to computer science. He was a natural athlete, although small for his age, and ran much faster than boys older than himself and won all the Middle School prizes. He had the family charm, though his was more aggressive than the others and he got upset if there was no reaction to his efforts. Neither of the boys had Kilen's steadiness.

In the end affection, good sense and the boys' wishes prevailed. Samreth stayed until he finished his studies here and Houssara has remained with us. His rapport with computers is nothing less than brilliant. He is now *consulente* (trouble shooter really) for an ever growing group of clients. It is almost like having a doctor in the family – he gets calls for advice and help at all hours. He has just been responsible for the installation of a complicated new communication system connecting the University and the Observatory of Florence to the biggest hospital complex in Tuscany.

The immigration papers were complicated and abysmally bureaucratic but we finally managed them. Kilen and I went to Genoa, the closest American Consulate where she could be 'processed'. It was a three-hour drive, during which we both indulged ourselves in the mixture of tears and excitement that marked the months we had to wait until she actually left. In Genoa we stayed at a small, respectable hotel within walking distance of the Consulate. I decided we must have a grand celebratory dinner but after what seemed hours of searching, we ended up eating Nouvelle Cuisine (or the Genoese idea of it), which left us considerably poorer and still hungry. 'Memorable' was Kilen's description of that night.

We arrived at the Consulate before it opened the next morning and found that the 'processing' would take all day. It did, although most of the day was spent in killing time from one appointment to the next. We walked around and around the not very interesting zone where the Consulate was, we squeezed each other's hands, chattered about nothing in particular and somehow the time passed. There was one particularly considerate member of staff, a young and attractive Italian woman, who allayed Kilen's fears a bit. The Consulate doctor, seeing Kilen's nervousness, allowed me to stay with her during the physical examination, which was a big help. The Consul himself was efficient and kind when we finally got to his office, the last moment in a tense and tedious day. He congratulated Kilen and told her she had gained a great deal: she answered 'We shall see.'

After Kilen and I had finished with the Consul, we went to a Genoese 'alimentari', stocked up on local delicacies such as *torta pasqualina* (a Genoese Easter cake made with artichokes) and *Cima* (stuffed, cold breast of veal) and drove home, arriving just as John and the boys were finishing dinner. John gave Kilen a huge embrace and she and Samreth both began to sob.

Kilen was the only one of the children who was neither frightened nor intimidated by America. Puzzled, curious perhaps, but always certain of how she felt and of her right to express herself. It was as though she had vowed to herself that she would set her own standards, make her own rules, determine her own behaviour. She somehow managed to keep America and American values at arm's length. Kilen knew, from bitter experience, that men are not naturally good: she was never guilty of the dishonest rationalizations she deplored. She observed (carefully and dispassionately): she interpreted. She never confused the two. I suppose that is why she loves the country more than the others do.

On Samreth's first trip to America he was cheated out of his wages. He had taken a temporary job picking grapes but after a month when he expected to be paid he was told that he had no proper papers and couldn't possibly expect to be paid like an American. Since he had, in fact, no proper papers, he had no recourse. Houssara was even more upset on his first trip when he approached a group of fellow ten- and eleven-year-old boys on a playground only to be turned away for being 'not American'. Young as he was he recognized this as a synonym for 'white'. He said that during his almost two-month visit the only white people who talked to him were in the shops. Coming as he did from the small friendly zone where we live, this was a shock.

Transatlantic telephone calls, the occasional letter and the even rarer visit kept us informed and aware of Kilen's progress. She has employed those extraordinary hands as a dental assistant and has worked, happily, for the same dental surgeon for eight years now. By hard work, frugality and steadfastness she bought her own house. Sary wanted her to marry 'within the culture', so she submitted to a series of courtships by fellow Cambodians. A stunningly beautiful Cambodian virgin with a steady, well paying job, who owned her own house in a pleasant area of San Francisco, was what my mother would have called 'a catch'. Many attempted. Not a single one came anywhere near success. Once she lost patience with a bumbling, terrified suitor and said 'Let's not waste time, what do you offer?' Sary despaired. Then she met Gary. After a rather tumultuous engagement they married in 1993. She is blissfully happy in her marriage. Gary is a Japanese-American whose father was interned during World War II. His widowed mother has preserved many of the traditions, or at least what we think of as the traditions, of Japan, where she was born. She is a meticulous housekeeper, a devoted mother and grandmother, a talented gardener and speaks very little English after forty years in California. Gary is attractive, honourable and just right for Kilen. Last year she produced a gorgeous, healthy boy whom I call 'The Samurai'.

When Samreth had *fatto la Maturità* (passed his Baccalaureate) with above average marks, we cast about for further educational possibilities. He had been to see his mother and sisters the summer before and found what seemed to be an admirable solution. The San Francisco College of Art offered a three-year course with a degree in such subjects as industrial design, book illustration, advertising and so on, and, as all such colleges do, dangled promises of work after graduation. We all agreed on the choice, said we would pay the tuition if he could support himself, and after bureaucratic wrangles about documents, he went off. He completed the course satisfactorily. I have a photograph of him in mortarboard and robe at his graduation – the only unattractive photo of him I have ever seen. His fellow students seem intent on the proceedings while Samreth looks out at the camera as if to say, as he often does 'What could I do?' The promised jobs were few and more than once the promised wage was not paid. He tried several different things and places. At one time he found himself in Texas where he had gone for a promised design job, and where he ended up shining shoes to get enough money to go back to California. Small wonder that when he discovered, almost by accident, he had a talent for salesmanship, he was pleased. He still has an impressive portfolio of his designs and showed it to me with justifiable pride but he realizes that selling Hondas brings in more needed money than designs.

A letter from Poutherein told me that Sary's husband was not an educated man like her father and when in Cambodia he had been a professional soldier (for the Khmer Serei). He was also, in the Southeast Asian tradition, an inveterate gambler. Therefore I was not unduly surprised when Sary divorced him. She kept the green card and is now an American citizen. Belonging in the bureaucratic sense was not enough for her, even the common memories she shared with her fellow refugees were not enough. The friendship with the other victims she found in California was not enough either. The new life in America seemed to have little effect on her, as it was a world so distant from anything she had ever known and believed in. She couldn't, wouldn't measure herself against these new experiences, conditions for success or failure no longer existed for her. That they existed for her children was all she wished. What she needed for herself was security and solace. She had no use for a 'clever God', one who wrote and said things she couldn't understand in a language not her own. What she wanted was something to which she could give her full and impassioned attention, to the exclusion of all thoughts about herself, her past and her problems. What she yearned for was a protective presence, to keep her from drowning. Buddhism made no promises, particularly Theravada as practised in Cambodia (only a Buddhist monk could achieve Nirvana), nor did it make any threats which seemed somehow important to her. She needed assurance. She never knew where she stood, within Theravada the system of merits and demerits was never made clear. Her old beliefs were still strong and the mixture led her in the direction she felt she must go. Her dreams became visions, her constant companion and protector, Christ, her favorite phrase 'In the name of Jesus'. She became a born-again Christian and in true matriarchal fashion took her entire family with her into the Voice of Pentecost Church.

When tragedy struck the family yet again, Sary's faith helped enormously. Poutherein's husband Chap Tim, father of her two children, was diagnosed with lung cancer. 'But this is America,' said a bewildered Poutherein. 'How can this happen here?' The cancer was brutal but quick and Chap died a few months later. He was forty-two. Samreth rang me in tears with the news of Chap's death. 'When did it happen?' I asked. 'About ten minutes ago,' he said, and hung up.

They had all lived together in the house bought by Kilen and Poutherein as the two fully employed members of the family. Samreth had just come to California to go to Art School, Poutherein's children (Mary and her brother David) were in elementary school. Sary was not able to work as she suffered from fainting spells, so she stayed at home and attended to the day to day running of the house. Chap was a goldsmith and had his workshop at home so that he and Sary spent a great deal of time together. As far as it was possible to ascertain, Chap had no family left alive. He became dependent on Sary. She began to teach him to read and write Cambodian, which he had never learned. Their attachment to each other was strong and shortly before he was taken to the hospital Chap was baptized in the bathtub giving great comfort to Sary and, I trust, to the others as well. As a Buddhist Sary had dreams of gold. As a Christian, she told me, she had visions and saw great swathes of purple cloth with the outline of a figure inside them.

After a long and painful period of mourning Poutherein began to smile again. She had interrupted her work as an accountant only briefly and the demands of a daily routine and two enchanting children to raise brought her back to her old self. Last year she married her former boss. Her husband is a fine-looking, blond American who towers over them all like a gentle giant. The children adore him.

Trinh, Tuyen and Bo prosper. They have had their troubles, too, but the troubles for the most part had little to do with exile. Last year Trinh and Tuyen opened the first Vietnamese restaurant in Tuscany. The hours are long, the work hard and there is considerable strain but they are established now and are, justifiably, proud of what they have accomplished.

A few years ago, after a bureaucratic hassle, we brought over Trinh's youngest sister, the only unmarried one. Lively, intelligent and full of natural charm she is a great help at the restaurant. She is now engaged to the chef whose name (Phuk) is always good for a giggle.

Bo does very well at the Liceo Scientifico. His marks are good under a demanding educational system, his friends are many, his tastes, for the most part, are Italian. He has just turned eighteen and is tall and handsome. I realized just how grown up he was when he received a notice to report for a physical examination for military service. He and Houssara have grown up as brothers, quarrels and all. They are, most of the time, devoted to each other.

Recently I called on Don Luigi whom I hadn't seen in years. He had been transferred to a Parish north of the city in a working-class suburb quite a distance from us. His church, San Martino, is not a tourist attraction and is in the town of Brozzi, a medieval *borgata* with fortifications constructed to protect the north side of Florence from invasion. There are a few traces of the old walls left, impressive even as ruins. San Martino and the cemetery nearby were begun in the eleventh century and suffered various restorations and serious damages during the Florence flood of 1966. The actual damages have all been repaired, the aesthetic ones have not. The Bell Tower rebuilt in the Renaissance still stands, untouched and unruined, as well as two Romanesque doors together with the splendid cypress grove. The Parish house is large, spotless and sunny: the courtyard a jumbled jungle of growing things. Don Luigi looked much the same as he had some seventeen years ago although he seems even larger (taller not heavier) than I remembered. He has a wonderful voice, gentle and powerful at the same time, useful in his profession no doubt. He no longer wears the *soutane* but was dressed in what the Italians call 'clergyman' trousers. I noticed with pleasure a slight vanity: he practiced what is known as the *riporto* – some long strands of hair combed over to hide a bald spot. We reminisced with mounting pleasure. The arrival and placement of the Asian refugees was the period of his greatest happiness he told me. He had taken care of over two hundred and swears there was not a negative experience in the lot. His Parish house is now home to six

Italian children that have been given over to his care (aged six to twenty-one). What began with the Oriental refugees has given him a vocation within a vocation. Priests are often described as 'serene', Don Luigi is more.

EPILOGUE

IF THIS WAS a story with a moral it would have a particular kind of ending, just to teach us our lesson. In fact the story is more complicated than that, it doesn't really have an ending. Whatever purpose or plan we might have had, the reality was, as it tends to be, different.

I wanted to hear more of their stories and perhaps tell some in their own words. I wanted to see at first hand how they coped with the contradictory colossus that is America. With this in mind I flew to San Francisco in February. When I arrived, after an eleven-hour flight non-stop from Paris, I was still dazed by the time change and Veuve Cliquot (I had flown Air France). To my delight and surprise, Samreth was waiting for me. He looked wonderful, handsome as ever and no longer vulnerable in Western clothes, a little heavier or perhaps just more mature. With him were his year-old son, his wife and her mother: the mother spoke no discernible English; the wife a few phrases; the baby had the romantic, deep-eyed beauty of his father. Samreth took charge of my luggage and me with admirable efficiency and in no time at all we were in his shiny new Honda on the way to Kilen's house, where I stayed and where Sary also lives. I met Gary, Kilen's husband, and the ten-month-old Samurai. I saw a great deal of Samreth and his wife and son and met Poutherein, her husband and children for the first time. How we talked and wept and talked. How clear the memories were. There were no longer the strange, and I suppose inevitable distortions that come from obsessive memories.

The past seemed at last, the past. Kilen confessed to me, in tears, that she had lied about her age. They all took wonderful care of me, Samreth took two days off work and guided me around the city; Sary made me Cambodian dishes that she knew I liked; Poutherein and Kilen took me to their favourite restaurants. I went to Church with Sary, Kilen and Poutherein on Sunday. I was passed from one to another with such thought and care for my wellbeing that I was touched.

We sat in the kitchen drinking innumerable cups of tea, talking and talking – of the past, of the promises kept and to be kept still. One night, returning from an elegant Cambodian restaurant (named, of course, 'Angkor Wat'), we all squeezed into the kitchen for our last cup of tea. Kilen began to sing and Samreth's wife began to cry. The tears were therapeutic, washing away the past to make room for newer wisdom. I could almost feel Sary's approval.

Samreth and Poutherein are on the surface more 'Americanized' than the others, although Samreth yearns to come back to Italy. He is, however, the only one who does. Samreth who played Bach and Mozart and read Dante now sells cars in San Jose, California. He does well financially, his natural charm has come in handy. His fellow salesmen tease him, I assumed good-naturedly, until Samreth told me there was nothing 'good-natured' in the jealousy he found surrounding him. The salesmen wonder how he does so well without speaking English any better than he does. Those without charm can never recognize its appeal, I suppose. He complains that he has no friends, no one to talk to about things that really interest him. He misses those long night sessions around the dinner table where the world was saved and set right. He misses his two great friends and his first great love and spends far too much money on transatlantic phone calls. Samreth had always been restless. He is married to a beautiful, silent, Cambodian girl: they married on the day after their son was born. His attachment to the baby is deep and his mother and sisters hope that, with time, he will settle. I have formed no opinion.

When the phone on my bedside table rings on Sunday mornings I know instinctively who it will be.